*Letters
to & from
My Soul*

Copyright © 2025 Emilie Lancour

All rights reserved. No information may be copied or distributed without the written permission of the author.
All contents of this book are based on my experiences, memories, and journal writing. There is no intent to harm. I am not a licensed therapist or medical provider.

Cover art by Emilie Lancour
Published by Hearts Unleashed Publishing House, Indiana
ISBN: 979-8-9882783-9-9 (Paperback)

First Edition 2025

Printed in the United States of America

[1. Journaling. 2. Writing Support. 3. Reflection. 4. Self-Help. 5. Mental Health Support.]

# Letters to & from My Soul

Emilie Lancour

## Dedication

To all the past versions of my soul,
here is what you needed to hear.

## Introduction

As I spent time reflecting on who I am and who I have been, these letters and poems poured out of me into my journal. These are the words I needed to hear from or say to some of the most influential people throughout my life, the people who loved me and affected how I see myself today. Many of the people are not here to say these words today. Some of them are the voices I hear in my own head. A few of them are from God and my intuition.

These are the words my soul is telling me now.
These are the words I needed.
Maybe I heard them and just needed the reminder.
Maybe they have been hidden deep inside.
It's time for them to be said aloud.

My hope is that reading these letters to and from MY soul will be a guide for you to write the letters to YOU and from YOUR soul.

You are the author of your life.
The stories from your past are real.
The stories about what is happening now can be real, too.
You can also tell yourself what the future will be.

Tell yourself what you need to hear.
Tell yourself what wasn't said.
Rewrite the stories that were harmful or painful.
Retell scenarios and situations from a different viewpoint.
Put in new characters or settings as needed.

Describe what the future will be.
Use the words to tell who you will be, what you will have, and what you will do.

Start each day with the story you need to hear.
End each day with rewriting what you don't need to remember.
Plan for how the story will be told tomorrow before you sleep.
Journaling can be healing and a way to process your thoughts and feelings.
Join me in getting your thoughts out of your head and onto paper.

Let's begin...

## Background Information

I was born to my mom and Bruce about two years after they were married. They divorced when I was around two years old. I spent a lot of time with my grandparents during this time. My mom then married a man named Rick when I was four years old. My two sisters were born when I was five and seven. Then, when I was nine, I was adopted by Rick, and he became who I called Dad. Bruce was in and out of my whole life due to depression and alcoholism. He passed away in 2015 when I was thirty-nine years old.

I married my high school sweetheart, Steve, after dating for five years. We raised three boys together and were married for twenty years. Steve unexpectedly passed away when we were forty-two. Two and a half years later, I started a relationship with Chris. We held a commitment ceremony in 2023.

Professionally, I was in the special education field for twenty-five years. I taught in a high school for two years, then middle school for eighteen, followed by five years at the local Intermediate School District. I retired at the age of forty-eight to start my own business. I own and operate Calm Water Writing, encouraging people to connect with their souls through journaling, especially those grieving. I have always been someone who uses writing to process my thoughts. I have published books and workbooks and created journals.

In the summer of 2024, I attended a conference where Matt Schmidt led a Quantum Healing session. During the meditation, we were asked to return to the moment we were born and have a conversation with our mother. While in the mediation, I knew my stories and poems needed to be in this book and that other letters to and from my soul would be written.

I knew I needed to be attending some sort of therapy again as well and wondered about EMDR. I asked a friend of mine, Zoe, a therapist, if she offered it or knew who did. She suggested that maybe parts therapy would be a good fit for me. It was strange at first to think of myself as many pieces all put together and that each part could have a different personality, need, and feeling in my body. I now see that some of my parts have names different from mine, and sometimes, I can see them represented by an animal or a color. Parts therapy has allowed me to learn about my past, which helps with healing, understanding, shifting perspective, and living in the present moment more often than I'd been doing. Each letter here is from a part of who I am or speaks to one of my parts.

I hope you enjoy and use this material as a guide for your own parts work and healing journey.

Dear Parts,

Hey everybody! Thanks for coming to therapy with me and Zoe, our therapist, today. I wasn't sure when I started therapy if I could separate the different aspects of who I am to be able to use this method to experience emotions and feelings to heal and understand myself. Feeling the sensations in my body, connecting with my emotions, and listening to Zoe's prompts has been and continues to be incredibly healing. I look forward to connecting with each of you again here around the dining room table.

Welcome Walter, you are one of my favorite parts, the logic part. I feel you control a lot of what I do, how I react, what fuels my anxiety, and what contributes to many of my different ADHD symptoms. I love that you want to keep me safe and secure, but I'm again going to ask that you hang out on the sidelines for a while so I can connect with my physical body and spirit, not just my thinking.

I am deeply concerned for you, teeny four-year-old Emy. I often see you sitting on the steps by the back door waiting and wondering. I can understand that you doubt your worthiness and wonder what you have done to be abandoned. I feel the emotions you're experiencing and connect with the panic in your chest. I often still experience it when I try to explain my anger to others.

Dear caretaker, I always see you protecting the people in my relationships and the other pieces of me. I have gained clarity about how your role has played out in my life as a teacher, daughter, mom, wife and partner, grief guide, and friend. It explains my interactions and selflessness. I know my continued work with you will also help me honor my needs and learn to care for myself too.

I'm honoring my love for you, little Layla. Seeing your need for support and knowing you are heard calms my anxiety. I want you to know that you can stand up and share your wants and needs without worrying that someone will get angry. It confirms why I try to ensure that everyone around me feels loved and cared for.

Being able to focus on mind, body, and spirit in a safe space and see how all of you and many other parts combine to make me the person I am today is comforting. Being aware of the sensations in my physical body is guiding me to better health. Choosing this method of therapy is allowing me to focus on my wants and needs while still providing love to those in my life.

I see each of you like a tiny strip that together make up a piece of licorice or as the individual clove that forms a head of garlic. You aren't a layer of an onion that's peeled off and thrown away. You are integrated and work together to make me into who I am.

Thank you!
Me

Dear Emilie,

Look at each part of yourself and give every part of you a big hug. Grant permission to stay if that part is supportive or permission to step back if it's not. Let every fiber of who you are have a say. Let this version of you guide the discussion, timing, and the parts.

See that you have access to all of who you fully are: the hurt, anger, confusion, feelings of abandonment, and at the same time, love, safety, support, and encouragement. Both of them always exist. Neither is bad or wrong. All of it is your makeup, the connections between your soul makeup and who you are meant to be. Your purpose is in your soul. You have always been on the right path. You are not meant to make all the decisions. You were chosen and loved. The shadow work can unlock your God-given gifts and purpose. You know your worth, abilities, and skills. Now believe that and trust that! Take time to focus on yourself, your wants, your dreams, your hopes, your desires, your love, your empathy, your understanding, and your compassion.

You matter! You are important! You are valuable! You are wanted and needed!

Love,
Your Soul Pieces

## What if I'm Not

What if I'm not...
good enough for her?
good enough for her daughter?
good enough to be a dad?
good enough to provide?
good enough to be in a relationship?
good enough to not stay single?
good enough to love with all my heart?
good enough to share my family?
good enough to stop some of my habits?
good enough for her?

What if I am?

To The Camp,

I want you to know that you are my space. The place I go when I need solitude and peace. The space that brings me joy. A place filled with memories. Where I can be fully me.

When I was little I spent so much time with you, in your building, on your beach, in your woods, walking down the driveway, swinging in your trees and swimming in your water. Now it is where I go when I need to reflect, grieve, be with God, feel the love of gramma and grandpa, spend time with family or connect with the water.

Inside the camp itself, I slept in both lofts. The first one being able to watch gramma and grandpa play cards and hear the fire crackling. The joy of being able to climb down the ladder in the morning to crawl into the hide-a bed with gramma because grandpa was already up and had the fire lit to warm the space. The second loft was a space of late night giggles with my sisters listening to the waves and foghorn through the open crank out windows and of being told to go to sleep from gramma down below.

I loved the fireplace built of rocks collected from your shore. I spent hours sitting on the stump watching the fire be built, having my feet washed to remove the blossoms in the spring or eating layers off of marshmallows on your hearth. The rocks grandpa collected are still lining the shelves on the sides of your chimney.

Gramma and I spent hours cooking, playing cards, picking agates, and making jam. I ate many of my favorite meals at your table using my specific dishes. The sandbox outside the door was a space for my creativity. The 'restaurant' I ran and operated, allowed me to use nature to create food, to connect with people and to be in control.

Your lake frontage is my favorite space on Earth. I have visited the

Atlantic Ocean in both North Carolina and in Florida, the Gulf of Mexico and the Pacific Ocean in Hawaii. I will always choose you over any other beach. The fresh cold water. The rocks including agates and omars. The countless hours spent in the water laughing with family. The incredible sunsets and northern light shows. And the view of endless water and continual beaches without people is priceless. But it's more than all of this. It's the feeling in my soul I get when I stand at the edge of the water and feel the movement of the waves, and the sun and wind on my face. It's the deep connection to something bigger than me. I experience pure peace and comfort here.

When I was little this was where I could escape. I could come to swing for hours. I could play in the sandbox. I could pick flowers and gather sticks. I could come to the beach and be away from all the worries, all the noise, all the people, any responsibility. I could choose what to do. Did I want to pick rocks, play in the sand, read a book, build a driftwood fort, collect birch bark for a fire, or walk to one of the creeks? I got to decide. Now this is where I return to because I still get to do these same things... decide, choose, be me.

I am so grateful that I have this space to myself when I need it. And that I am able to bring friends and family here too and share in the memories, the feeling and the comfort of you.

Thank you. Thank you for being my space, my comfort, my joy and my peace.

Love,
All Versions of Me

**The Camp**

woods
driveway
hill
lake
rocks
beach
loft
fireplace
birch trees
swingset

peace
comfort
serenity
joy
connection
memories
solitude
relaxation
happiness
love

**God's Recipe**

Leading by example
Old soul energy
Visionary
Light out of darkness
Helpful
Generosity
Positive change
Guiding
Inspiring
Listening

Dear baby,

Your mom told me yesterday that she's pregnant. I don't know what to do with that information. This was not part of the plan. I was supposed to finish school, get my degree, be able to be fully employed and have a job in an area I want.

Now everything is going to change with you on the way. I don't know how to support her. I think she's scared and excited, but I don't know if I'm excited yet. I don't know if I'm ready to be a dad and ready to parent with your mom. I don't know if we have similar ideas of how parenting and discipline are going to go.

I don't know how money is going to work. I don't know what this will do, and I don't know even what to think yet, but I've had a few hours to think about it and process it, and I don't want your life to end. I don't want this pregnancy to go away. I want to learn to fall in love with you and to see who you become in 9 months when you enter this world. I want to be a really good dad, be in your life, and love you. I want to continue loving your mom and growing in our relationship. I know that we have lots of support from family and friends. People will be just down the hall and down the street from us. They're going to help us on this journey by helping us learn how to be parents and love and care for a child.

The more I accept that this is reality and this is happening, the better I feel about it. I know that your mom is always going to have your back. She's already excited, even though this is unexpected and unplanned. It's going to derail a lot of the stuff that we thought we were going to be able to do as a young couple. We haven't been married that long. I know this is going to change a lot of things. I'm learning to be excited. I'm filled with anticipation of meeting you and seeing the type of person you grow up to be. I can't wait for my mom, dad, sisters, and nieces and nephews to meet and get to know you. I know you're going to be loved.

Love,
Daddy

**My Worth**

God-given
Inherent
Not able to lessen
Unconditional

Because I am here
Because God loved me
Because I'm human
Because of my soul

Allows me to love myself
Allows me to be confident
Allows me to learn and grow
Allows me to be me

Allows others to love me
Allows others to help out
Allows others to guide
Allows others to support me

Dear baby,

Wow! Just found out that I'm pregnant with you. I always thought I'd be a mom. I've watched other people become moms. I've watched how excited my mom was when my sister had my three nieces.

I don't know if you will be a boy or a girl. I don't know what life holds for us, but I'm so excited to be your mom. I can't wait to go through this pregnancy and get to meet you at the end. I am so excited that this has happened, and I'm absolutely terrified. I don't know if I know how to be a mom, but I've been around kids. I know the basics. I know how pregnancy works, but I don't know about being a mom and helping raise a child.

I don't know how your dad is going to accept this and if he's going to be ready for this, or what's going to happen. I don't know what conversations are going to come up, but I'm going to fight for you, and I'm going to keep you. I'm going to care for you during this pregnancy and for the rest of my life. I hope that when I tell your dad this news, he will also be super excited. I also hope he's a little scared, too, because I want to be able to do this together. We can teach each other different things. We can build off of each other's strengths. I know the caring man he is, how he's involved with other things, and how he's always willing to help.

I know that when my mom and dad hear the news, they will be excited and a little scared because I'm their little girl. I don't know if they're ready for me to be a mom now. They are already grandparents to three amazing grandchildren, and I think they've always wanted more. I know that they're going to be a part of your life with them living so close by. I hope that they are accepting of this pregnancy and ready to help me raise you, care for you, teach you and be there for you.

As a teacher, I have a loving heart. I think we both do, and we can share that with you when you come out into this world. I'm excited for the day that I feel you kick, and I want to hear your heartbeat. I know that this precious little life is going to be mine and that I will get to watch you grow up. Maybe someday you'll be a mom or dad of your own and I will get to help carry on that joy and that skill of raising children.

I want you to know that you are loved here on day one. You are loved. You are wanted. You are beautiful. This is a miracle. No matter what happens, what you do, what you look like, what size you are, what you want to be when you grow up, what relationships you're in, what skills you learn, I am going to love you because I'm your mom.

Love,
Mommy

**When Was I Chosen?**

Not for mom to be pregnant
Not for the divorce
Not for the adoption
Not for the move
Not for Steve to go out with me
Not to be a widow
Not to be a single parent
Not for Chris to go out with me

Not aborted
Not divorced
Adopted
New friends
Asked me to prom
Always in love
Still a parent
Put his arm around me

I was chosen

---

*In what situations were you chosen?*
*In what situations were you not chosen?*
*How did these situations/relationships affect you?*

Little Baby Emy,

I think I'm done. We're separating, and we have fallen out of love with each other for many different reasons, but you're not one of them! We are getting divorced, not living together, and not being a married couple anymore, and it has nothing to do with you. You are the one reason we have talked about staying together, but we know that's not the reason. We need to separate and be ourselves to love you the best we can. Right now, that means we have to be apart.

You will still spend time with both of us. You'll live with me, but you'll see your dad a lot. He loves you. I love you. Both of our families love you. This is not your fault. It is not anything you have done. It is not because you were born. It is not because of the time, energy, or money that we invest in you. It's not you.

It's us. We can no longer function in a marriage. Someday, maybe you'll understand how hard it is to lose somebody you've been in love with and that you love. I hope you don't. I hope you find love and keep love for your whole life.

There are a lot of changes that are going to happen if he's not living here anymore. We may find somewhere different to live. He's going to find somewhere different to live. You'll spend time in both of those places. You'll still get to spend time with both sets of grandparents. Both of us are going to continue to take care of you and love you. We will provide for your needs because you're worth it.

Love,
Mommy (2 years old)

**To Do List**

See the gold that fills the cracks.
See the sun that's always there.

Smell the frankincense to be guided.
Listen to your heart and intuition.

Feel the love of God.
Feel the support of others.

Touch your hearts to feel the beat.
Touch your chest to feel your breath.

Hear the silence, the message, the voice.
Hear your dreams come true.

Trust the sensation and knowing.
Believe the path is paved.

Accept the help that's offered.
Follow your heart and intuition.

## 16 – Emilie Lancour

Emy,

I am struggling to know who I am. I've decided that I can't be in a marriage with your mom. I can't be the dad you need me to be. I need to do some soul-searching. I need to figure out this grief that I've been dealing with losing my brother and my sister, the hard things my parents went through, and the things that my other sisters went through. I'm figuring out who I am now that I didn't get to finish college, and I've been working for your grandpa. I've been trying to heal this relationship with your mom, and right now, I can't do it.

I hope you know that even when I'm not around I think about you and I love you. I want to be a part of your life but I can't figure it out. I don't know how to give love to multiple people. I don't know how to love who I am. I feel like I'm failing you because I'm not around and I couldn't stick around. I couldn't make the marriage work. We struggled and we divorced.

I'm afraid of how much that's hurting you even though you're little and you're young, and you probably don't remember the days without me or the days with me. I'm sorry if that's changing who you are and your feelings toward yourself, but I love you. You were the best thing that's happened to me in my whole life. I thought growing up, I had unforgettable memories. I thought being with my mom, dad, and siblings was incredible. I thought being around my nieces and nephews when they were little and being a part of their lives was amazing. I thought going to college and meeting new people was terrific. I thought falling in love with your mom and our wedding day were fantastic.

But none of that compares to the day you were born. You came into this world because it changed who I am. It changed my identity. Your birth and your life have made me a dad and a father, and I want to be there for you. I want to help you grow. I want to make great memories with you. I want to share my family with you. I want to sing you lullabies, read stories, take you on car rides, teach you to listen to music, and introduce you to good food. I want all of those things for you. I want to attend events when you go to school, on a team, or in a club in high school. I want to be there when you fall in love. I want to be at your wedding and walk you down the aisle someday. I want to be a grandpa if you choose to have your own kids.

I want all of those things, but most of all, I want you to know that you're loved. I want you to know that you're worthy. I want you to know that nothing I do is meant to hurt you. The times I can't be around are because of my depression, and it's led me to alcohol. I know that's not the solution, but I don't know what else to do. I thank God daily for bringing you into my life because you give me hope. You give me a reason to be here and a reason to stay. I don't know how to be there for you every day when I no longer live in your house. I don't want anything to happen to you when you're with me, and so if there are days that I am not feeling good or I have drank too much. I'm not in a good place. I am not going to come and see you because I don't want you to experience that, to be a part of it, and to have anything ever harm you.

I want you to be happy and experience joy. I want you to spend time with your mom and family and connect with my family. I want you in my life. I need you to know who I am as a dad. I want to be a good dad to you because you deserve it. I love you, kiddo.

Love,
Dad

**How Old?**

How old do you have to be to feel responsible for everyone's happiness?
How old do you have to be to feel unloved or unwanted?
How old do you have to be to see being home as hard and unwanted?

How old do you have to be to feel absolutely loved and protected?
How old do you have to be to move forward and feel loved?
How old do you have to be to feel wanted and worthy?
How old do you have to be to know your heart and soul?

Emilie,

Hey, I met your mom a few nights ago, and one of the first things she told me was that she had a daughter. That's okay. I don't know how deep into this relationship I will get, but knowing that she is also a mom just makes her that much more beautiful. Her willingness to share that and risk getting to know me further shows a lot of strength and courage, and with only knowing her for a little bit, she strikes me as the type of person who's passing that on to you.

I spent a little bit of time with you today, and I want you to know that even though you're really young, you have a lot of personality, and I can tell that you're going to be somebody who loves to laugh and that you're open and welcoming and accepting of whoever you meet. You don't know me at all, and yet you were willing to share your toys with me and sit by me. I hope if your mom and I build a relationship, I can also build one with you.

From,
Rick

**Licorice**

Every part of your soul was given to you by God
Each piece is woven together like a string of licorice
If it were examined, tiny frays would be visible
The pieces of damage made you strong and resilient
Focus on all of the parts you have been given
Reflect on the frays as a way to understand with compassion
You are woven into one piece, so you're not easily broken
You can be stretched, twisted, turned and still stay you

---

*What message do you want/need to hear from a higher power?*

Little Emy,

I love that you want to be at our house. I love getting to help raise you and seeing you change, grow, and become more beautiful and fun every day. I love that you like to spend time here. I love holding you, reading to you, and giving you a bath, but I think I most love taking you into the blue room, sitting down in the rocking chair, wrapping you in a blanket, and singing lullabies to you. I love the feeling of you in my arms.

I know that you are safe and protected right now, and you are loved. I know you feel that because of how your body relaxes and curls into mine. The unconditional love that you have for me as your grandma comes through. When I held your mom when she was a baby, I felt that connection and that love; it was so amazing. I am so lucky that I get to do that again with you. I am so thankful your mom lives close to us, needs me in her life, and lets me be a part of your growing-up years. I'm so happy that Grandpa and I are able to have you be here during the days and to spend the nights. We like being able to help your mom when she's working, going to school, or just needing time for herself. I love that you feel comfortable here and that you seem to want to be here even though you're very little.

I want you to know that you are always welcome here. This will always be a safe and loving space for you. There will always be food for you to eat, activities for you to do in a space that you can get rest and sleep in. Grandpa and I will always do what we can to help you out. You are such an amazing little girl. We are so blessed to get to spend time with you, to love you, to help you grow, and to see the person you're changing into.

Love,
Gramma

## Music

Lullabies by my mom and grandma when I was little
- to help me sleep

Request on the radio and the top 40 on weekends
- to fill the room

Played at school dances, prom, and mom prom with friends
- for so much fun

Always on in the car, and song is dependent on my mood
- to improve the ride

My words written in personalized songs
- to help my boy sleep at night

The words of scripture and matching them to instruments
- hymns as prayers

Mixed the memories together of our songs and favorite artists
- to help with grief

The words are often more important than the tune or the beat
- to focus on the lyrics

Music with a fun beat with movement and dance
- used to move my body

---

*What role has music played in your life?*
*How are you affected/impacted by music in your life?*

Emy,

Where are you going to stay tonight? Are you going to come home? Are you going to stay here at Grandma and Grandpa's?

I see you sitting on the steps, trying to decide. Neither Grandma nor I care where you stay tonight. If you want to come home, you can return in the morning. If you're going to stay here, you can come home in the morning. Neither one of us will feel unloved or unwanted if you choose to stay at the other place.

I know you love staying here with Grandma and Grandpa. I know how special Grandma makes you feel when you're here as an only child. I know that you're loved and taken care of here. I will be okay if I go home without you tonight. I will still love you if you choose to stay here instead of coming home tonight. I will love you even if you stay for breakfast and lunch tomorrow and stay another night. But also know that you are welcome to come home. I am happy to have you there tonight. I can bring you back in the morning or tomorrow afternoon, but you need to make a decision.

And you can make a decision. You need to do what you want to do. What is your heart telling you you want to do? Don't worry about how I will feel or how Grandma and Grandpa will feel when you make your decision. Just follow your heart!

Love,
Mom

24 – Emilie Lancour

Dearest Emy,

Scooch over and let me sit by you for a minute.

I can see how much you're struggling with trying to decide if you want to stay here or if you want to go home tonight. Grandpa and I are happy to have you stay here. You are always welcome here, but I won't feel abandoned, unloved, or hurt if you choose to go home tonight. Grandpa or I can come down and get you in the morning or your mom will walk you up here or your dad will bring you over. If you don't stay tonight, you could stay tomorrow night. Your mom won't be mad if you want to stay here. I won't be mad if you want to go home.

If you want to stay here, you just need to say good night, tell your mom you love her, and let her go home. We will make some chocolate pudding and play a card game. You can take a bath later, and we'll finish reading the "Bobbsey Twin" book that we're in the middle of. In the morning you can have breakfast. I can make you French toast. I can take you home, or if you want to stay for lunchtime, you can do that too. It's all up to you. You get to decide. Because your mom is tired, going home and going to bed would be okay. I am going to be up for a while.

If you want to just stay here, you won't be loved any less based on your decision. You are worthy of making a decision based on what's happening in your heart and not worrying about judgment or fearing that somebody will be hurt when you make a decision.

Love,
Gramma

## Grandpa

The sound of
Berries landing in the peanut butter bucket
The chainsaw cutting down the trees
The news hour playing on Friday night
Your tongue cleaning your teeth

The smell of
Bug spray on your green coveralls
Peanut butter sandwiches for lunch
Bleach on your t-shirt worn as a nightgown
Thimbleberry jam cooking on the stove
A fire at the camp on a cold morning
Dove soap because it floats

The feel of
Your large but soft hands
The hard caramel in a frozen candy bar
The wind while riding in the back of the truck
The cold Grandpa rocks in the creek
Crumpled newspaper to start the fire
The worn spots on the steering wheel

---

*What message do you want/need to hear from your grandparents?*

Gramma and Mom,

I want to stay. I don't want to go home, watch TV, and sleep in the bedroom with the scary image in the corner. I don't want to listen to a baby cry. I want to stay here at gramma's.

Gramma, I want to be spoiled. I want to have a frozen Milky Way with Grandpa. I want to play cards with you in the dining room after we clean up the dinner dishes. I want to take a shower, use the little shower, and then have you dry my hair. I want you to tuck me in with the pink blanket with the satin edge and read to me from The Wizard of Oz. I want to fall asleep with my feet tucked in the bottom of one of Grandpa's t-shirts.

I want to sneak downstairs in the morning and see how far I can get before either of you notices that I'm awake and coming downstairs. I want to help you make me homemade French toast. I want to get one of the little cinnamon candies to have as my pill when I drink my cup of mostly milk, with a teeny bit of coffee, while you have yours.

Love,
Emy

**Comforting Little Me**

Eating chocolate pudding while playing rummy
Running a restaurant out of my sandbox
Operating a pretend card company with my sisters
Choosing the color yellow and teddy bears
Lying on my stomach in the water
Picking agates with the sun on my back
Falling asleep to the sound of the fog horn
Cuddled up in the loft of the camp
Feeling the wind in my hair as I rode my bike
Teaching my stuffed animals math on my porch
Using my camera to take pictures of the sunset
Having music on twenty-four-seven
Sometimes, the same song on repeat
Writing all of my thoughts in a journal
Reading with a flashlight under the blankets
Making sure the closet doors were closed
Playing in the tub, ending with a hair wash

———————————————————

*What do you find comforting?*

**Stay at Grandma's**

I was loved either way.
Gramma didn't care.
Mom didn't care.
They both loved me.
If I stayed or if I went.
I could decide.
I could choose.
It would be okay.
I would be okay.
I could change my mind.
I would be loved either way.

**What if She Chooses**

I see the little girl.
She's sitting on the steps.
Her eyes are crying.
She can't decide.
She wants both.
She doesn't want to hurt anyone.
Does she stay or go?
What if somebody is angry?
What if somebody feels hurt?
What if somebody feels left out?
What if?
What if?
What if?

I see a little girl.
She's sitting on the steps.
Her face is smiling.
She's decided.
She wants both.
She wants to make herself happy.
She chooses.
She decides.
No one will be angry.
No one will be hurt.
No one will judge her.
What if she chooses joy?
What if she follows her heart?
What if she feels so loved?
What if?
What if?
What if?

Dear Emy,

I want you to know that I'm really worried that if something happens to me like I'm in a car accident or I was to get cancer, the courts would award custody to your dad. This would mean you would not be living here with Rick, the man who has been raising you, and your sisters anymore.

I've approached your dad and asked him to sign some papers that would allow Rick to adopt you. I want you to be happy. I want you to stay in this house where you are loved, cared for, and connected. I want you to grow up with your sisters. Although they're your half sisters that's not how they've ever been treated or you've ever been treated because that's not what family is. Family doesn't matter about the genetic component and who shares genes and blood. It's about who spends time together and who makes memories together.

I'm offering him the option to still have custody of you and be able to see you when he's able to and when he is in town and feeling good. I don't want to cut him out of your life. I just need security that you are going to be taken care of and that you can have a really good life, and I'm not sure that would continue to happen because of what the courts would do if I were gone.

This is a really really hard decision for me and Rick. We have talked about it a lot. He's willing to sign the papers to adopt you and legally make you his daughter. He already feels like you're his. He takes care of you already. He loves you already. He knows you're a part of his life forever. No matter what happens with us, you would be a part of his life. He is raising you as his daughter just as much as he's raising your sisters. He wants you to be safe, feel loved, and know that you have a place in this family. I hope that Bruce will sign the granting of giving up his parental rights so that that security is there for you. I hope he knows I'm not trying to cut him off from you, change your opinion of him, or ruin the relationship that you do have. I hope that he can still see you, spend time with you, and create memories. I want him to see you grow and learn and become the best version you can be. But for my sake, I need to know that you will be loved and taken care of, supported, and connected with the family you live with every day.

Love,
Mom

## Adoption

Because of love
Because of family
Because of fear
Because of safety
Because of security
Because of worry
Because of love

Dear Emy,

Your mom approached me about signing some papers, and I really don't know what to do about it. I know that if she were to die, I would have full custody of you. You would live with me, move in with me, bring your stuff with me, and we would build that life, but I don't know if I could do that with the place I'm in right now. I don't know if I can be a full-time parent. I don't know if I have the skills, the time, the energy, and the mental health to be able to care for you and love you in the way that you deserve and in the way that you're getting that right now.

I know absolutely how much your mom loves you. She's loved you since day one, maybe even before day one. And she's going to love you always for the rest of your life no matter what happens to her, with us, with her and Rick, your sisters, your grandparents, or with me, she's going to always love you. She has given you an amazing life. She lets you be you. She encourages you to be independent. She wants you to make choices and decisions and to learn. She wants you to be in your home. She wants you to be with Rick. She wants you to be with your sisters. I get that.

And I am battling depression. I am battling being stuck grieving. I am struggling with relationships, how to be loving, and how to commit to a marriage. I don't know what job I'm going to have. I don't know where I'm going to be living. Right now, I can't take care of you and be the dad you need with the custody schedule we already have worked up. I can't provide for you financially. I can't provide for you emotionally. I can't provide a stable home life for you. I can't provide you with siblings. I can't provide you with a step-parent. Your mom has done those things. She provides all she can for you and reaches out to others when she needs more support, like your grandma and grandpa.

Although she said that I can still see you and have a life with you, I'm afraid we're going to grow apart. I'm afraid I won't get to build more memories with you, and I won't be able to be your dad still if I sign these papers. But I'm more worried about what would happen to you and our relationship if I had full custody. So, I think I'm going to sign the paper that relinquishes my rights to be your dad. I know I'm doing it because I'm giving you a better life than I can provide right now.

I know how loved you are at home. I know that you're provided for. I know you're getting meals and birthday parties and holidays. I know you have friends over and connections at school. I know how close you are to your grandma and grandpa and how much you need them to be in your life as well. I know you've connected with Rick's family and that they love you too. How couldn't they? You are growing up into such a beautiful person.

I want you to know that this decision is not easy. I've gone back and forth so many times. I want you to know that no matter what I decide, it's not because of who you are or anything you've done. You are exactly the daughter I've needed. You make me smile so much when you come to my house, and we do things like making salt ornaments at Christmas, or you walk around the edge of the water bed and fall into the middle in laughter or take gum out of the candy jar drawer. I love how when we drive to Grandma and Grandpa's house, you sing along to songs on the radio, how 'Uptown Girl' is one of your favorite songs, and how you love hamburgers and french fries. I love your connection with my parents, siblings, nieces, and nephews, and I don't want any of that to change. I want you to be loved by them. I want them to always be a part of your life.

I'm afraid that this little piece of paper will change all that, and you don't deserve that change. You are worthy of being loved by everyone you come in contact with. You deserve to feel worthy. You are wanted. I never want you to feel abandoned. I never want you to feel that you caused me to stop loving you. Because I will never ever ever ever ever no matter what happens. I will always always love you. You will always, no matter what anybody says, no matter what your mom says, no matter what Rick says, no matter what your grandparents say, no matter what the lawyers and the jury or the courts or the law say. You will always be my daughter, and I will always be your dad.

You are so innocent in all of this situation and I know there's been decisions that you've had to make and I know it's hard but I want you to know that I believe in love. I loved your mom so much and although I was nervous and scared and unsure I fell so deeply in love with you the moment you were brought back into the room at the hospital. I've loved every moment of the last 9 years of your life. I cannot love another person with as much love as I feel for you. There's a different connection between a parent and a child than there is between anybody else in the world and that connection that I've made with you is one of the most treasured parts of my life.

I want nothing but the best for you. I want you to grow up with amazing experiences and amazing memories. I want you to live in a loving home and attend a great school and learn everything you can. I want you to know how beautiful you are. I want you to know that you will always be my dear little dolly no matter what the papers and the law say. You are loved. You are worthy. You are unbroken. You are wanted. You are not being abandoned.

Everyone is in this situation because of the love they have for you and the hopes and dreams they have for the life we all want you to be living. Everyone wants you to be happy. Everyone wants you to grow emotionally, physically, and spiritually into the incredible woman we know you're going to be. I always want to be a part of your life. But right now I can't be that person. I have days where I know God is telling me to figure stuff out because it's hurting you. I know that people are upset with me because of how I have treated you and my inconsistency in your life. I know my mom is angry. So maybe if I make this official and know that it's only for a worst case scenario. Because losing your mom anytime in your life but especially now would not be healthy for you. And then to be grieving and in that space and have to leave the family that you're growing with would not be fair to anyone especially you.

So I'm making a decision out of love. I'm making a decision based on what you deserve. I'm choosing your life over mine and I think that that's what my job as a dad is. To always choose you. So although I'm giving up my rights as being your dad on paper, I will always be your dad in your heart. I will always love you. I will always want to be involved. I will always be proud of you. And I want you to always feel loved, wanted and taken care of. I love you, kiddo.

Love,
Dad

**No Pretense**

I am and have always been loved.
I never was or will be abandoned.
I can grow from my past without living there.
I can have trust in the future without fears and worries.
I am present here now, able to love and live.
I don't need to pretend.

---

*What did you need/want to hear from your father?*

Dear 48-year-old me,

You are not too young. You are not too crazy. You are not making the wrong decision. You must follow your heart, intuition, and belief in yourself. It's about time you're doing this. Leaning in and following what society says you should do and would be the easiest and the best for you doesn't have anything to do with what your soul knows you need. If you need to leave teaching and retire and start something completely different because your heart is calling you to do that, then you retire!

If your body is telling you you need movement and stretching every day, then move your body! If you want to continue to support your kids even though they're not little anymore, then support them! If you don't want to spend time with certain people in certain places, then don't go to those places or be with those people! If you don't want to follow a schedule and get up every morning at 6:30 to have time before work, then don't! If you want to start your own business and earn an income because you have talents, ideas, things to share, and a story to tell, then do it!

You have to get over worrying about the judgment from other people. Most people don't care, and not in a mean way but they have their own things that they're worrying about and are struggling with and are trying to do and dreams that they're following. They don't have time to worry about what you're doing and how it's going to affect them. Most of what you want to do isn't going to affect anyone in any way other than you. You can be replaced at work. Your children have skills, knowledge, and ideas, and they are smart, so they're able to figure things out.

You can make financial decisions, and you have made successful financial decisions before. You are worthy of following your dreams. You are worthy of believing in yourself. You are loved by so many people and have been since the minute you were born. God made you for a purpose. Your purpose is teaching! You have wanted to be a teacher since you were very little, and you ran a fake school on your front porch. You wanted to be a teacher throughout elementary school, especially when working with amazing teachers and mentors. You wanted to be a teacher all throughout college as you earned your degree. You wanted to be a teacher when you taught high school and middle school and worked for the ISD. You still want to be a teacher. You have skills and knowledge to teach others and if that's what your heart says you should be doing, then that's what you should be doing.

You can't let comments from other people tell you how to live your life. No one has the right to discourage you from following your dreams, believing in your intuition, or knowing God's plan and path for you. You get to decide. You get to make decisions. You get to know what you want. You can feel what's right for your mind, body, and spirit. You, and only you, can decide what you need, want, and deserve. Your choices allow your children, family, friends, colleagues, and strangers to see what's possible. To see that you can make decisions that might seem selfish to others but lights you up. Your choices allow others to make their choices and follow their dreams. Your story might be the survival guide that someone else needs. You matter. Your story matters. Your life matters.

Love,
Your Soul

**40 years**

decisions were made
out of love
out of care
because I was worthy
because of family
because of connection
because I was wanted

everyone had a choice
but me
too little
too young
not meant to

decisions were made
for the best
for a better life
for a home
for love
for me

Dear Emilie,

It bothers me to think that you don't trust yourself or believe you are worthy. When I create a soul, that soul is made 100% worthy and 100% perfect. It is made to be in a specific body at a specific time to have a specific experience. I put your soul in your body to live your journey because I wanted you to affect the world you're living in right now.

I needed you to hold people together. I need you so that others feel loved and wanted and never abandoned. I have given you a strong soul that even death hasn't broken. There may be some cracks and some weak spots, but they never break.

You are whole, loved, and wanted. Your life matters. Your soul speaks to you, and you were made to listen. You are meant to share your skills, talents, and stories with others so they, too, can have faith, experience joy, and feel healed from the things that are hard in life.

I have given every single human being a soul and the option to make choices. You were never meant to make your choices based on anybody else but what was deep inside of you. You were never created to make your parents happy or your siblings happy. You were not made to make a partner happy or your children happy. You were put here to be happy. You were meant to be in relationships with your family, friends, and loved ones. Relationships and connections make you happy, but their happiness can't be at the expense of your own happiness.

You need to trust my plan. I know you've been angry and confused at times with the plan I've laid out in front of you but you've always survived. You've always healed. You've always been able to experience joy. You are an empathic healer because of the soul I gave you and the experiences you've had in this human life. Because of the things you have witnessed and felt deep in your heart and soul, it allows you to share them with others.

I see how that lights up because of your faith in me and your trust in your purpose. I see you smile when someone reaches out. I see the love and amazement you have for your kids. I deeply feel the losses you've experienced. I understand your anger and appreciate your confusion because I know the whole story. I know that if you choose yourself and you put your wants, needs, and desires before that of anyone else, you will follow the path that I created when I put your soul in your human body. You will continue to connect, collaborate, and share with so many people worldwide because they need you.

But you can't fill them up, help them, guide them, teach them if you don't feel good about who you are and you don't trust that you deserve to be happy. You need to speak your truth no matter what the words are going to make someone else feel like. You may tell someone something, and they get angry, or they leave you, or they tell you things back that are hurtful. But as you know, everyone has a story, and everyone comes from a different experience, and maybe they are not on the same journey that you are on. You have incredible patience when it comes to people who are hurt or have been hurt. Your way of being is a light. You guide others out of the darkness. Your ability to see people where they are and offer them your story of where you've been and how you've got to where you are now and your dreams of where you want to be allows them to also heal and experience joy, peace, and love.

I'm not even mad at the choices you make. I gave everyone the ability to choose. I have unconditional love for you and unconditional love means that I can never stop loving you no matter what decision you make or choice you follow or dreams you have. This also means that when I see you experiencing something positive, it lights me up too. When you see one of your boys being successful or laughing or helping somebody, it sparks a little more light in your heart, knowing the people they are becoming. I feel that when you choose you.

The people in your life have made a choice to be there. Your parents chose to have you come into this world. Your dad chose you to be one of his own. Your family has loved you, accepted you, and cheered you on. You have friends that you've known for forty-five years who still will be by your side. Your love for Steve will never end, even though he chose to follow me when I asked him to. Chris has chosen to love you, knowing you have a background, because everyone does. Your children choose to be at home and to spend time with you because they know you're never going to abandon them, even if you choose to do things for yourself. Even if people disagree with the choices you're making or they think they're crazy or ridiculous or scary or wrong, you get to pick! Knowing that what you choose always has the foundation of love makes them the right choice.

You have to make sure that you keep your foundation strong to build different parts of your heart and make room for the rest of the people you are meant to love. Your heart needs to be healthy in order to grow. You make yourself healthy by learning your voice of intuition and hearing what your soul is speaking to you. I created you out of love. You live out of love. You will die in love. Love is the only answer there is to any decision.

Love,
God

**God made me...**

Worthy
Lovable
Kind
Empathetic

An author
A writer
A photographer
A creator

A water lover
A sunset lover
A person lover
A journal lover

A mom
A daughter
A granddaughter
An auntie

A heart
A soul
A mind
A spirit

---

*Who were you made to be?*

Dear student,

I appreciate that you shared with me that you cheated when you were in high school, but you need to get over it. I had my purpose for what I talked about, and not everything that teachers share with students is meant for every student. You know that as a teacher. Not every kid needs to learn geography or math or how to spell. You didn't need to learn that specific poem that you chose not to memorize. But I was also teaching you the skill of memorization and the ability to do homework and do hard things.

Had you gotten caught and failed that assignment and maybe even failed that semester, you still would have gone on to graduate and gone on to college and became a teacher. That risk you took seemed huge, but in the grand scheme of things, it meant nothing. It didn't offend me as a teacher. It wasn't a huge disappointment to your parents.

What made you decide that you would not memorize many lines of text from some old dead person? You probably had something much more important to do that evening then spend time memorizing. You made the best choice for yourself at that time with what you knew. That's all that's ever asked of you.

Your teacher

**Role of the Student**

To speak up
To try new things
To understand
To discuss
To experience
To never give up
To take time

**Everyone**

Everyone questions.
Everyone believes.
Everyone learns.
Everyone experiences.
Everyone is on a journey.
Everyone has a past.
Everyone is doing the best they can.
Everyone has a different definition of love.
Everyone experiences emotions differently.
Everyone connects with different people.
Everyone celebrates in a different way.
Everyone needs love, empathy, and acceptance.

Emilie,

I knew you liked me. I knew if I had asked you out, you would have said yes. I liked you, too, but I never felt good enough for you. You were liked by everyone. You had this amazing, outgoing personality. You were smart. You're beautiful. You fit in everywhere. And I never felt like I fit in.

I didn't feel like I was somebody you could bring home. I apologize for the times I led you on or made you think there could be something. I was struggling with what to do, who I was, and who I wanted to be with, and I'm sorry if you got hurt in that situation.

I am so glad you found somebody with a solid background and a great personality who matches so much of your being. Someone else who was outgoing and didn't have a group because you fit in everywhere. You both were on sports teams, did academic pieces, and were involved with student council and prom committees. You were active in your church, and you had terrific families you grew up with. You both had goals, dreams, and hopes. I see your love, and I'm so happy for you.

I'm sad for myself that I didn't have the courage to ask you out and to try a relationship with you.

Your crush

**Inspire**

Inspire
New growth
Success
Partnership
Intertwined
Relationship
Encourage

---

*Is there someone in your past that caused some heartbreak?*
*What do you think/hope they would say to you today?*

Em,

I can't offer you a cure to stop crying every day. But I can tell you it's because your heart is so big. You want everyone in your life to be okay, happy, never hurt, and never feel unworthy. Your desire for the world to be a peaceful place where nobody is damaged or made to feel abandoned is taking a toll on your body. Your heart grows so much and is so big that I think it makes your eyes leak tears because, deep down, you know that you can't fix everything for everyone.

Your feelings of unworthiness and undeserving of love conflict with how your heart feels being in friendships and a relationship. You cry because you're so overwhelmed with feeling everything for everyone and not feeling enough for yourself. You need to journal more. You need to share your journals with others so they can see the hurt, pain, and confusion you feel about who you are, what you're meant to do, and how you're struggling with feeling undeserving of love from anyone. Suppose you can see that you were made to be worthy. You love to give love because of who you are, not what you've done or what you're going to do or who's been in and out of your life. I think the tears will stop being as consistent, and they'll be tears of healing, not tears of fear.

Love,
Your broken heart

**Unwilling and Willing**

Unwilling
to be the best-kept secret
to live in fear and worry
to continue feeling unworthy
to worry about judgment
to let my past define me now

Willing
to move forward
to let go of my pain and suffering
to promote my experiences
to share my story
to believe in myself
to know I'm worthy
to follow my intuition

## 52 – Emilie Lancour

Emilie,

I chose you because I watched you for months. I watched you want to be with somebody else. I watched you laugh, smile, tell jokes, and tease people. I watched you help others in any situation. I watched you be part of a team. I watched your faith when we were at church together. I watched how you acted around your family, my family, and others. I saw the teamwork you did on committees. I had so much fun with you when we would go to the movies, play pool, hang out at Burger King, go for car rides, and listen to music. I felt the love you gave to everybody, and I wanted that for myself. I also knew you were somebody who had dreams and that was going to go far in life. And not to mention that I thought you were super sexy, attractive, beautiful, and pretty all at the same time.

I was so angry when you got that rose because I had not found the courage to ask you out yet, and that person should have known that you were not interested in them. You had never hung out with them. You didn't do activities or anything in school with them other than sit by them in the study hall. That anger made me realize that I needed to ask you to prom. I was so excited when you said that you would go, but at that time, I didn't know that you thought we were going as friends. I was already falling for you at that point.

I want you to know how grateful I am that you pulled over at my house that day, parked on the side of the road, and waited for me to come over to your window to find out why you were there. I am so glad you said no to seeing Fern Valley but yes to seeing "Fern Gully." I am so happy that you were willing to go to the movies alone with me and not bring all of our friends along.

I remember how nervous I was picking you up for prom that night. Meeting your dad, meeting your mom, not knowing which house was yours, and thinking about the fact that I was in love with you already.

I was so scared during that dance that when I whispered in your ear that I loved you, you were going to walk away. I was so afraid that you wouldn't say it back because you didn't mean it or you didn't know it. But I felt a super strong connection between us. We had known each other for so many years between the school and church and the community. Being in classes together, being on the prom committee, the hours we spent after school, time spent in religious ed classes, and time out with friends, that was worth the risk to tell you. I didn't expect you to say it back and so when you didn't, I wasn't surprised. I'm so glad that your reaction was to just put your head on my shoulder and continue dancing and not leave me there.

And the next night, when you ended our phone call by saying that you loved me, that was in my top 10 moments of my life. I felt nothing but love every time I saw you in a hallway, waiting in line to get on the bus after school, on stage for some swim team pep assembly, when I got to be part of a group project in English class, or when we worked together on our decade project for history. I loved spending all summer together and our senior year with plans for the future.

I knew our relationship was strong enough to survive long distance for college. I was so proud of you for choosing to go on to college to become a teacher and to live that dream. I love that you wanted to come home on weekends to see me and be with me. It made me so happy that you were willing to spend time with my family and allowed me to spend time with your family because family was so important for both of us. It would have been tough if we had had to choose one or the other. I loved that we could talk about anything together whether it was faith or love or background stuff or things in school or stuff with our friends.

And the thing I appreciate the most is that you always let me be me; you let me talk about cars, radios, stereos, Detroit Tiger baseball, football, or even politics; things that I knew you had no interest in. But you would listen because it was important to me, and therefore, it was important to you. Your ability to have empathy and sympathy for what others are going through is incredible, and it's one of the biggest things I love about you.

Love,
Me (Steve freshman year of college)

**Love Is**

Love is…
Love is both hard and easy.
Love is confusing.
Love is commitment.
Love is forever.
Love is strong.
Love is a soul emotion.
Love is a connection.
Love involves trust.
Love involves helping.
Love involves compassion.
Love includes empathy.
Love can be expressed differently.
Love is never wrong.

---

*What conversation do you want to have with your first love?*
*What words do you wish you had said to them?*
*What would you like/need to hear from your first love or significant other?*

Steve,

I am so sorry that I have stained your shoulder almost every night for months. I don't know what's wrong with me. But you are one of the only people I can be honest with about my feelings and emotions. I am so grateful you allow me to write out what I'm thinking and that you're willing to read, process, and talk through things with me.

I have so many fears about being abandoned, and I'm constantly afraid that I'm going to say or do something that's going to make you leave, walk away, and break up with me. I fear that if I push you to do things that you're not ready for because I am, you'll get mad, and that I'll get hurt. I'm constantly worried about saying the right thing and being honest with you, which hurts me. I get headaches and an upset stomach because I don't want to lose your love. I want you forever. I need you to want to be with me physically, emotionally, and spiritually. I want you to pick me up and see me every night. But I don't always tell you because I know you have other things you want to do, like hang out with other people, be home with your family, or even just sit and watch TV in your underwear. Sometimes, I still struggle to believe that you chose me, asked me out, that you want to be with me, that you find me attractive, and that you don't think I'm too loud, outgoing, or sensual.

I want you to know that my background of not consistently feeling loved and wanted affects me daily. I worry that friends are going to stop liking me. Or that teachers will tell me I'm not smart enough because it's happened. Or that someone at church will get upset with me because of my thoughts and ideas, which might be different. Or that your family will find stuff wrong with me and convince you to end our dating relationship. I fear that my mom worries about me spending as much time with you as I do and if that's good or healthy. I don't think she understands it because I finally have somebody who wants to be all in and see all parts of my life. I am so appreciative that you want me in your life. You want to be with me and see we have a future together, even if I have to write it down in a note. Eventually, I will get the courage to tell you more because of the number of things I've shared that didn't upset you or make you leave.

Love,
Emilie (high school senior year)

**BE and FORGET**

BE
Fun
Creative
Loving
Caring
Teaching
Alone
Writing
Together
Playing
Joy

FORGET
Safe
Normal
Permission
Self-doubt
Worry
Fear
Judgment
Chaos
Exhaustion
Busy

Emilie,

I said no to your proposal last night because it scared me. We're still in college. We do not even live in the same town. I don't know what's going to happen or where we're going to end up. Although I love you and know that I want to be with you forever, I'm not ready to make that commitment yet. Telling you no was scary because I know what you're thinking now. You think that I don't want you, that you're not good enough for me, that you shouldn't have said anything, that you were wrong, and that I'm mad and that now because you said that, I'm upset. I am not upset that you asked me to marry you!

I am so excited that you want to spend the rest of your life with me. You believe in us that we can make it in a long-distance relationship and that someday we will live in a house together and we will be married. We will get to take our relationship further physically, and we will have all of those pieces. I'm so thrilled that you see that as our future, and even though I said no, I still want to be with you. I still love you. I'm not going anywhere.

And a little bit of me wants to be the one who proposes to you. I want to get a ring. I want to give that to you because you deserve it. It's tradition. And my grandpa would be so upset if he found out that I didn't get to be the one to propose.

I love you.

Love,
me (Steve, 1994)

**Will you Marry Me?**

Want to be together forever?
Want to say vows to each other?
Want to have our families witness?
Want to wear a tuxedo?

Want to be together forever?
What to make a permanent promise?
What to celebrate our love?
Want to wear a pretty dress?

It's not about the day
It's not about the clothes
It's not about the people
It's not about the words

It's about us
It's about the love
It's about the future
It's about forever

---

*What are your thoughts, beliefs and feelings about marriage?*
*Would sharing this with someone feel helpful? Who might that person be?*

Dear Insecurity,

I felt embarrassed that there was an attraction between me and another person. I absolutely 100% will be faithful in my marriage and would never interact in a way with someone else to damage the relationship that Steve and I have. But there's a portion of me that is sensually attracted to another person. This other person I know has feelings for me and won't act on them, making it hard to be in the same space. He admires my body. It feels good to have somebody else think I'm attractive. He likes to spend time with me and does different things to make that happen. I know he will not cross the boundary set based on our roles, but sometimes, the idea of being with another person is exciting and scary, making me question who I am. I enjoyed spending time with this person. I enjoy having somebody like me.

I have never been with anyone else other than Steve, and the idea that somebody else might want to be with me in that way made me feel good, and there's nothing wrong with that. Others might have considered the relationship that the two of us formed as inappropriate, but it was not. It helped boost my confidence. It made me feel loved and appreciated and wanted. It made me feel attractive and worthy of affection. It confirmed my love and commitment to Steve as well. It might have even added a little bit of extra to our marriage.

Love,
My Sensuality

**Sensuality**

Feel good
Be myself

Ask for what I want
Speak my truth

Share my desires
Know I'm attractive

Enjoy the real me
Love my reflection

Trust my body
Understand the beauty

Send out signals
Receive love

Make the sounds
Allow the movement

Feel Good
Be myself

**Garbage Day**

Throw out the need for perfection
Get rid of the need for permission
Toss away fear
Take out the anxiety and confusion
Put overthinking at the curb
Dispose of negative self-thoughts
Discard judgment of others
Unload self-doubt
Clear out wanting approval
Eliminate worry
Dump the need for how
Scrap the idea of unworthiness
Part with using only logic

---

*Practice writing a letter of kindness, gentleness, generosity, and understanding to yourself.*

Hey you,

If it weren't wrong, I would ask you out. I would show you how physically attracted I am to you. It's hard to be around you as often as I am and keep our relationship as friends. Most of what I started feeling for you was purely physical until I realized how much you actually cared for me and wanted what was best for me. The fact that you would go to bat for me with other people and share how smart I was and how much potential I had made me love you even more. I had to make some tough choices for myself, and leaving was challenging because of my family, but I also had to leave you.

Deep down, I knew it had to happen because there was nothing that I could do to be with you without breaking your heart. I know how much you value your marriage and the commitment you had made and that there was no way you were ever going to choose to jeopardize that to be with me. I often wondered if there was some attraction on your part.

You are attractive. You are an incredible mom and person. You are an amazing teacher and friend. Keep loving everyone the way you do.

Keep in touch! I will always be here for you.
Secret Admirer

**Desire**

I want you
Why can't you
I wish we could
I think about you
You are attractive
You are so beautiful
I love to be near you
I want more time with you
I love that you care about me
I love that you understand me
I love that you try to protect me

Emilie.

I forgive you for disconnecting from your soul. I forgive you for not knowing who you were meant to be and allowing that light to shine no matter who you are with. I forgive you for allowing the experiences that other people were having to influence how you felt you had to be. I forgive you for accepting the lies that you were told as truth. I forgive you for choosing to numb out and be extremely busy so you didn't have to process and think and feel all of the hard emotions. I forgive you for thinking you were unworthy. I forgive you for thinking you were too loud and too much. I forgive you for not using your voice to share your passions and purpose with the world. I forgive you for allowing fear to be your guide instead of trusting the process and God. I forgive you for not asking for help and feeling that you had to do everything alone. I forgive you for feeling unconfident about sharing your beliefs and choosing your own path. I forgive you for staying silent in relationships for fear of judgment.

Love,
Forgiveness

**Worthiness**

I am worthy.
I was born worthy.
My worthiness doesn't change.
I can't be unworthy.
I can't be less or more worthy.

My actions don't change my worthiness.
My thoughts don't change my worthiness.
Other beliefs don't change my worthiness.
My worth is not dependent on anything.

God made me worthy the moment I was created.
God chose me to be fully worthy of love and purpose.

I am worthy.
I was born worthy.
My worthiness doesn't change.
I can't be unworthy.
I can't be less or more worthy.

---

*What might you say to yourself in a letter of self forgiveness?*

Dearest Emilie,

You were never abandoned.

Being taken to the nursery at birth had nothing to do with you as a baby. The cord was around your neck, and you needed to be taken care of. Your mom wanted you back and missed not getting to hold you immediately.

Your mom did not abandon you by having you stay with your grandparents. She needed to figure out who she was in order to be the mom you needed. She knew you were loved and taken care of. She knew how special you felt being taken care of by them.

Bruce never abandoned you. He couldn't love you the way you needed him to, so he stayed away for your protection. His battles were his to fight and should not have caused you pain. You were not able to understand the situation because you were little and no one felt that it was your burden to carry. No one intended for you to feel that you were unworthy or that you were not wanted. The intention was for you to feel safe and to be loved. The depression and alcoholism that he was fighting was not anything to do with who you were as a person. He absolutely loved you and you were one of the reasons he was able to keep going. He loved you enough to stay away.

Steve did not leave you when he died. He did not go because of who you were or how you were as a wife or a parent. He left because it was part of God's plan. God needed him more than you did. God knew you would be okay. God knew that by losing him you would find your passion and be able to help others see that life can be a combination of grief and joy, love and memories and that by becoming a widow and a single parent forced you to learn who you are and who you have always been.

If something in your relationship happens now it won't be because of who you are as a person or how you are in your relationship. It will be because it is part of the plan, not because Chris will want to leave you. He does not want to ever hurt you. He does not want to ever see you sad or upset. He will stay as long as God allows him to.

Your children choosing to lead their lives and live as you have hoped does not mean they are abandoning you. The skills and lessons and love you have given them throughout their lives fuels the dreams they have and allows them to be the best versions of themselves. This has always been your hope and your dream for them. You need to let them be on their own and make decisions, and struggle, and have difficulties, even if that's hard for you. You know your strengths, skills, and knowledge about yourself when you're going through something extremely difficult. They're going to be okay. They know they always have a home with you. They know you will always love them. They know you would go out of your way to protect them and to keep them safe. But they're not you. They do not feel abandoned or unwanted. They have self-confidence and believe they are worthy of love because of how you raised them and the life they have lived.

When people leave your life, it is because they no longer need you to live out your dreams and purpose. Everyone stays as long as they are required. Friendships may last for a few months or years or your whole life.

Love,
Your Worth

**Abandoned**

Left behind
Left alone
Quiet and still

Left when angry
Walked away
Not want the fight

Never physical
Never bruises
Never blood

Alone
Scared
Worried

Hey Emilie!

Stop it! Stop worrying about what other people might say, think, or feel when you make a decision! You need to decide what to do, what to feel, where to be, or how to act based on your intuition, heart, and soul. Everyone is entitled to their opinions, experiences, and feelings. No one's worth is more than what your worth is. Everyone is created worthy. Everyone has self-love. Everyone is beautiful in their own way. Everyone has talents. You just need to see and believe that yours are perfect for where you are right now in life.

If you choose something because your soul says yes, no matter what anybody else experiences, it is right! When others hear your choice, it does not mean you are wrong or hurtful. Others in your life may have different emotions when you tell them what you've decided. Someone might feel angry, upset, sad, and maybe left out, but it doesn't mean your decision is wrong or that you shouldn't make it. Decide because it feels good in your heart. Decide because you can. Decide because you're a grown-up. Decide because of love for who you are. Loving yourself is not arrogant or selfish. Loving yourself allows you to then love others in return. You cannot fill up other people if you are empty.

Let others see you go for your dreams and live your life based on your purpose. Lots of them also live their lives and follow their dreams because they have seen you do it and know it's possible. Be an example for your children. Be an example for your friends. Be an example for your clients. Be an example for the community. Be an example for future generations.

When you are having difficulty picking something that you want, flip a coin. Often, when the coin is turning in the air, you will get a feeling of what you want to appear. That's your answer! Now go with it. Don't second-guess yourself. Don't worry about who else is going to be affected by it. Just choose what you think is right for you!

Love,
Decisions

**What's First is What's Honored**

If I choose to focus on joy, I feel joy
If I choose to read or write, I feel joy
If I am by the water, I feel joy
If I play a game with my kids, I feel joy
If I connect with others, I feel joy
If I use my voice to share, I feel joy
If I choose a healthy meal, I feel joy
If I make an intuitive decision, I feel joy

Greetings 9-year-old Emilie,

I am going to finalize your adoption. Mostly because I don't think anything in your life is going to change. You are going to still be loved by three amazing parents who want what's best for you in all situations, but especially if you were to lose your mom. The choice to have this adoption go through means that you will always be connected with your sisters and have that life.

Legally this changes who your father is but that doesn't mean that you can't continue to have a relationship with Bruce. It doesn't mean that he loves you any less. In fact, the meetings I've had with him tells me how much he has struggled with making this decision but the fact is he's doing it because of who you are and how he wants you to live.

Your mom's coming forward with this choice also shows how much you are wanted and how much of a life she wants you to have where you can feel loved, supported, and safe.

Rick's adoption of you absolutely shows how much love somebody can have for a person who's not related. Family means more than blood.

As a family court judge, I make the best decisions I can to help families. The first person I consider in every decision is the child. I feel like this is the best decision that could be made right now, given the knowledge we have of everyone involved. All any of us can do is use the information we have and follow our hearts. May you continue to feel the love of all of these people. May you feel wanted, seen, and heard.

Sincerely,
Judge K

| Are you... | Or are you... |
|---|---|
| garbage | treasure |
| debris | prize |
| rubbish | jam |
| junk | pearl |
| dust | trove |
| litter | catch |
| sewage | jewel |
| trash | goody |
| useless material | valuable |
| rubble | worthy |
| waste | find |
| refuse | precious |
| dead wood | premium |
| scrap | blessing |
| riffraff | benefit |
| remains | gift |

Dear Mom,

You do an incredible job as a mom. Your ability to see multiple sides of a situation has made it really hard for you to make decisions and know what is right, but it's also what has made you an incredible parent. You are able to see what you grew up with and understand what Dad grew up with while seeing three other individuals with the skills and personalities we have made all aspects of raising children hard. It may make discipline difficult when you don't agree. It made child care a hard choice when there were differences. Deciding about seemingly simplistic things like meals and chores became long discussions.

You have always wanted us to grow up and be able to be independent. For us to be able to be in a relationship and to potentially have our own children. You wanted us to have the skills and knowledge to function in a household and at a job, and in society. Your desire for us to never feel abandoned or unworthy caused you a lot of suffering and pain that was unnecessary. Holding us as babies, singing us songs, tucking us in at night, teaching us pieces of our academics, and supporting us in our free time and athletics and other clubs, showed us that we were and are worthy. Your lack of judgment allowed us to grow close to you and share our lives with you. Your prayers and protection have allowed us to feel loved and safe. You have done an incredible job providing for us as a single parent. You and dad did a phenomenal job raising us into the young men we are today. We are men who help our community, are friends with each other, want to be with family, and show love.

When you were told that one of the reasons we have done okay with the loss of our dad is because of how much love we felt between the ages of zero and six is true. The love and support and guidance that you and Dad provided for our entire lives have taught us to feel worthy of love. To know that we are supported and guided. It has been amazing to understand anger and frustration and to know that no matter what we do, experience, or say, we will be loved. Unconditionally loving us has been the biggest gift you could ever provide to the world. Allowing us to see you struggle and grieve gave us permission to struggle and grieve.

Now you must give us the permission to dream and follow our hearts. Allow us to see you get what you want and do what you know is right. Share with us your successes and lessons and wins. Let us see you be in love with yourself. Let us be independent. You have filled our toolboxes and now allow us to create and use the tools. We will not feel abandoned. We will only feel loved.

Love,
Your Children

**Living with Intention**

Not so many hard, fast goals
What I want to do to be the best me
Focus on the adjectives and feelings
Be more present so as not to worry
More of what I like to do every day
Time spent with those I love
Trust my gut and intuition
Follow my heart and dreams
Believe that my purpose is defined
Saying yes to the version of me that lights me up

---

*What do you need to hear as a parent from your child(ren)?*

Emilie,

I know you're worried that I'm going to leave you because of something you say or do or what your body looks like. I know you don't think you're a great wife or mom. I know you worry about every student in your classroom and the colleagues that you work with. I know you put my needs before your own.

None of these things are true.

I chose you, knowing what you looked like, what you weighed, and your athletic abilities. I chose you because of your personality and the type of person you are when you're with others. I chose you because of how much you love and how hard you work to make sure others are happy.

When we became parents, it just showed me how much more worthy you were of love. I know that you absolutely would do anything for those boys. I know you put them before our marriage and before me, and I'm okay with it because I know that our love is super strong. I know we're going to be together for life. I see how hard you work to keep this house going and to keep our boys feeling wanted, safe, and loved at all times. I know you struggle with discipline and chores because you don't want them to ever suffer or do anything that's hard. But I also know you can see my point of wanting them to someday be able to be a dad or a spouse and that these are things they need to learn as they're growing up.

I love the time we spend together alone, whether it's going for a ride or on Sunday mornings. I love that even though you have to write everything down first, we can have great conversations and share our thoughts, dreams, frustrations, hopes, and fears with each other. I'm sorry you spent so many nights not sleeping because you were worried about finances. I wish you could have shared with me what was going on in your head and that you didn't fear that you were going to be a failure for letting me know. You are extremely smart and intelligent. I am always amazed at the knowledge you have and the things that you have learned and what you're interested in. I love your ability to read, write, and share.

Although I've never witnessed you in the classroom I know you are a phenomenal teacher because of the stories you share about the students you work with and the pain that is experienced when things are horrible for them, but you can't save everyone.

You need to focus on you sometimes. You fill the schedule with all kinds of things but you need to take time just for you to go and sit by the lake or to drive around and take pictures. You can take a bath and skip the dishes. I'm not going to love you any less if you choose to do things that don't make anybody else happy but you. I go fishing or hunting, and it doesn't affect anybody else. You need to do those same things. No one will be mad at you if you want to take an hour to yourself every day or go on a retreat on a weekend. We got this. We can function without you, and that would be okay. I won't feel left behind. I won't feel that you're being selfish.

I feel so blessed to be in this marriage and parenting journey with you. I am so glad that God brought us together way back in high school and that he's allowed us to grow in our relationship. I am grateful that we have both an emotional and physical relationship. I am blessed to have somebody who puts up with my sense of humor and my teasing. I know it's an honor to have somebody who wants to be with me when I'm in the shape I'm in. I appreciate all you do to keep this family together and keep this household running.

I love you now and forever.

Love,
Steve

**Marriage**

lifelong commitment
unconditional love
a team around the house
honest and trustworthy
plans for the future
live and vacation together
make decisions together
share unapologetically
intimacy between souls

Em,

I had a little bit of an inkling that something was going to happen when I had the surgery. I was nervous, scared, and worried, yet my belief in God told me that everything would be okay. I'm glad you were able to go to work and that my dad was able to be here. I always joked with you after being with your family when your grandma was dying that I didn't want anybody with me because I didn't want people laughing and joking.

But I didn't need anybody with me because it was quick and easy. I was not in any pain when it happened. It was an easy decision because I've always known that heaven is where I was meant to be. I knew that angels were carrying me to God and that it was going to be okay. That my pain was going to end and everything was going to be healed. My scars and wounds from the surgery would be healed. My wrists, shoulders, and back would no longer hurt. My weight would not be a concern.

I did question how everybody was going to grieve my loss, but I also knew I had to go. It was my time. This was all part of the plan from the very beginning. I know you are going to be okay. I know the boys are going to be okay. I know my family is going to be okay. Everyone is going to come together and be on a grief journey together, even though each person will have a unique experience. I know that everyone's faith is going to be huge. I also know that it's going to be tested. You might be angry with God for choosing to take me away from you, but you'll always have the memories and the connection to me.

No matter what you choose to do and if you go forward, I will always always be watching over you and the boys. I will leave you all the signs that I'm okay and that I'm here. I will watch the boys graduate and be in relationships. I will watch you grow and become a different version. I will always love you. I have loved you since I was sixteen. I was so happy you were somebody I could share all parts of my life with, including my faith and my beliefs, and you always accepted me for them, even if it was different from your own.

God has a plan for each of us, and right now, His plan for me is to be a guardian angel. I don't know what that looks like or how it's going to happen, but it's what I need to do. I need to be with you only in spirit now.

I think deep down, I knew that something was going to happen because I spent time with each of the boys individually, and you and I have had some incredible conversations and experiences lately. I have ended commitments and shared my thoughts with other people. You and I have talked about what would happen if I were to pass away. You know what you need to do as far as finances and running the household. You are an amazing mom and have those skills. Your knowledge of grief and healing is going to be so supportive to not only the boys but to so many other people. I know you're going to spend days and hours crying because of how much you already cry, but I've seen an improvement in that. I feel like you're starting to process things more with words than tears.

Continue believing that God has got you. He has an absolute plan for each one of us and I'm excited to watch you live out more of your plan. I can't wait to watch the boys continue to grow up and develop into the men we've helped raise. I am so proud of the people and friends they are. I am happy they love each other and get along and can tease each other and laugh. Make sure you take care of yourself while you're taking care of them.

Maybe it's time you start asking for help and accepting that others can provide for you and be there for you, and it doesn't make you a failure or weak. I know you've always struggled with making decisions but I think now you will be forced to make them on your own, and that will help you see your worthiness. You are the love of my lifetime, and I will always be right here waiting for you. Here's a quarter; call someone who cares. Suck it up, buttercup.

Love,
Steve (a few days after I passed away)

**Grief is...**

Grief is a weird thing.
Grief really sucks most of the time.
Grief is weird because it's so individualized.
Grief has no rules or timelines.
Grief for each person can be different.

Grief doesn't have to be every moment of each day.
It can come and go throughout your life.

Grief is a reminder that you love someone.
Grief can make you smile as you remember something.
Grief can bring you together with other people.
Grief might last a lifetime.
Grief is different and unique for each situation.

---

*What messages do you need to receive from a loved one that has passed away?*
*What do you wish you had said to them?*

**Grief Journey**

There's the shock! And the disbelief!
How can this be? Maybe it's a nightmare?
But I'm awake! How are you gone?
How are you not here?

What will happen now?
Who do I need to call, and why does it have to be me?
I want to be alone, but please don't go away!
I don't know how to decide.

Thank you for being here. I know you're grieving too.
We've got this! We've made it before.
It's hard, scary and confusing.
I know we're together, though.

You do you, and I'll do me.
We'll all get through this in our own way.
Sometimes, I need to yell and scream and cry.
Sometimes, I need to smile and laugh.
Do it all with me when you're ready!

Today, I feel him. I know he's here with me.
He'll never go away.
No matter how many tears I shed, the songs I listen to,
or the stories I tell myself, I'll always feel the love.
I'll always have the memories.
I choose the good ones now, not the sad or
the scary ones of the day you left.

It's time. It's time to let go. The fear. The worry.
The loneliness. The confusion. The hurt. The anger.
And let all of them sink to the bottom of the lake.
They can stay there. Not seen.
Not present, yet always there because it happened.

I choose joy. I choose love. I choose to smile. I choose to share.
I choose to tell the story of how I got here,
how I threw the rocks of grieving into the lake out of my backpack.
I'm done carrying them. I'm filling the backpack with light,
with love, with a sign, a smile, a laugh, a wink.

Grieving is over.
The deepness, the darkness,
the ongoing sadness, the shock,
anger, and confusion.

Grief will always be in my back pocket,
ready for those unexpected moments like the grocery store.
And the ones we know, like dates, weddings, and procedures.

But joy is here, too. All around.
In the love I have. The memories of who I was.
The time we shared. The smiles you gave me.
You can't and won't go away, and for that, I'm grateful.
For that, I know I can be okay.

Emilie,

I think it's funny that you don't remember ever meeting Chris. I checked him out for you years ago when we played hockey together and hung out at Sunday school. I knew someday he'd be important in your life.

I am totally okay with you loving him and being in love with him. I watch you with him. I see how happy he can make you. I see the love that's shared between the two of you, and I just know that you have always had enough love to give to everyone. I know and believe that your love for him is different from the love you had for me and yet I see the similarities.

I see how you want him to be happy. I know you need the physical and emotional relationship that he can provide. I'm so thankful you found somebody else who has gone through grief and allows you to do the grieving that you need to do. I'm glad you found somebody who accepts you for who you are and finds you beautiful.

I also want you to know that if he ever does anything to hurt you, so many people will defend you, and I will haunt him. But I don't ever see that happening. He is a good man. He has an amazing heart and an incredible amount of love for you. You have been so good for him. You have helped him come out of his shadow and to feel confident. He had been waiting for someone to love and take care of him. He was tired of being alone. He was jealous of others in his life having marriages and relationships. He was hurt by the relationship he had and knew that it had to be different. He has that with you. He has unconditional love, and he knows it. He doesn't ever want you to be hurt or sad or upset, just like I didn't. He tries hard to understand what you're thinking and going through, but he struggles because he sees you as amazing, beautiful, smart, kind, and loving. He wishes you could see the you that he sees. I wish you could see the you that I see.

Let him love you. Let him take care of you. Make decisions. Tell him what you want. Don't be afraid to share all of you with him. He's got you. He'll always love you. Nothing you can say or do will change the love he feels for you. He wants you to feel loved and to feel wanted. He wants to give you everything that you deserve, whether you've got that figured out yet or not. He's yours for the rest of his life.

Watching you figure out that you were ready to try loving somebody else was really hard because I thought we'd have 60 years together or more. I know we had plans to do so many more things together as husband and wife and as parents. I believed we would someday renew our vows because it was something you thought was important; even though I agreed with my grandpa and knew that I had said it once, it meant it. I am grateful that you found somebody to commit to love for the rest of your lives. Both Chris and I feel honored that you have gotten tattoos out of your love for us.

He has struggled with how much you loved me and continues to do so, but he also knows that that's made you into the person that he fell in love with. He loves every part of you. The parts that you also love and the parts that you feel are broken.

Don't fear sharing who you are with him. He is strong enough and has enough love to handle anything you tell him about who you are, who you want to be, and what you want.

I knew the other people in your life were not right for you. I knew the people that ghosted you were only there to teach you that you were ready. I watched you navigate these situations and it broke my heart that you were sad and upset, but I also knew that Chris was going to come into your life when you were both ready for a long-term lifetime relationship.

I will always love you and watch over you, although there are some scenes that I choose not to watch.

It's not surprising that you chose somebody who lets you be you, lets you be a mom, and lets you be in your family and in his. You know that you need somebody who will listen to you, love you unconditionally, be with you physically, and want the forever story.

Continue changing and growing together. You were meant to be. You and I were meant to be. As you always said, your heart just grows a new space when you need to fall in love again.

Love,
Steve (about Chris)

**You're Too Young**

You're too young to retire, they say
Well, I am also too young for other things

I'm too young to be a widow
I'm too young to have my mortgage paid
I'm too young to be a single mom
I'm too young to be unhappy
I'm too young to be stuck in grief
I'm too young to live in fear
I'm too young to not fulfill my dreams
I'm too young to waste my mornings

**Connection**

Today we connected
Today was fun
Today was unknown
Today was freeing

I'm still not sure
I'm still grieving
I'm still a widow
I'm still a single mom

I'd love to see you again
I liked your arm around me
I think about maybe kissing you
I wonder if this is too fast

What did you think?
Did I talk too much?
Was it all about me?
Are you ready for more?

Em,

I want to understand what you've gone through in your entire life that has made you this person that you are today. I want to hear your feelings and try to understand what that means for you now. I only want you to be happy. You deserve to be happy. Everyone does. I want you to feel comfortable telling me anything or sharing everything with me. I won't judge anything you tell me. Your experience is your experience.

I don't ever want you to feel afraid of how I'm going to react if you say something. I don't ever want you to keep things bottled up inside because you're worried. I like being able to give you things and do things with you that you want to do. I'm used to getting up and getting things, so it's not a big deal when you want something but don't want to go to the kitchen. I'm happy to pay for things when we go out because I think it's a way of taking care of you. I think you deserve to be taken care of.

When you're with me, I want you to be you. You don't have to be a mom. You don't have to be a leader. You don't have to answer to anybody or feel unworthy. I love you, and I always will. No matter what you tell me or what you do, that isn't going to change. I don't care what you weigh or what you eat, or the choices you make about your health. I will help you with the decisions you make.

I'm glad you do things with your friends, kids, and family. I'm glad you're okay with me doing things with my friends and family. I think it's healthy for us both to have time by ourselves. It doesn't make me angry when you feel you need to be a mom or auntie. It doesn't upset me when you choose to go out of town or plan events. I don't get angry when you do things that make you happy. I want you to be around for a really long time. I love you, all of you!

Love,
Chris

## The Waters I Swim In

I swim in some deep waters
Waters of self-doubt, unworthiness, and confusion
Sometimes, I'm drowning in the waters
With fear of abandonment and being unloved

I'm learning to leave the beach and join the lake
Where I can feel included, loved, and wanted
I know that water is a metaphor for safety
Peace and calm even when the waves are crashing

I know how to swim
I know how to float
I know how to open my eyes underwater
I know how to hold my breath

Being in the water allows worry to be released
The waves let the fear float away
Just be me if even for only a few moments

When I feel I'm floating, I can be aware
I can put my feet back down and touch the bottom
I know that when I'm busy, I can float
When I get tired, I can take a breath

I can sometimes be by myself
I don't have to worry about others safety
I can trust the lifeguards
I can just enjoy the water

Dear Emilie,

Your soul is incredible. Your soul can be trusted. Your soul only wants you to do what's best for you. I love the way you honor your soul through journaling, SoulCollage®, prayer, meditation, being by the water, healing experiences, and making choices. People choose to connect with you because of how deeply your soul feels love. Your soul is an amazing color of green and leads from the heart. Knowing what you feel in your heart is the path you're supposed to follow.

Your body is incredible. You are tall and beautiful. Your smile is amazing and contagious. Your eyes light up when you get excited. Your breasts are part of what makes you attractive. Your long legs give you your height. Your weight does not affect how people see you or love you. There are things related to your body that could be changed, like choosing more protein and less sugar, balancing your hormones, and keeping your cholesterol normal. Honoring your body with things like stretching, drinking water, eating fruits and vegetables, going for walks, doing yoga, and getting enough sleep and rest shows your physical health is important to you.

Your mind is incredible. The amount of work you have done to heal from your past and to learn to love yourself is amazing. Your ability to teach others skills and empathy while going through so much yourself is phenomenal. Your mind is unique. Your way of processing things through writing and poetry is creative and honoring who you are. Doing things like journaling, bullet journaling, meditation, relaxation and breathing, talk therapy, prayer, teaching, creating and hobbies like reading and coloring allow others to see how self-care can be beneficial for not only the mind but also your body and spirit.

Continue to focus on all three. Your mind, body, and spirit all need to be honored daily. Connect with others. Ask for support. Allow people to assist you in deciding what you need. Healing all three parts of who you are will take time and a lot of effort, but the rewards of having a strong mind, body, and spirit outweigh the pain and fear that you might be experiencing as you think about making this journey.

Love,
Your Mind, Body, and Spirit

**Self-Care**

How do I need to take care of myself mentally?
How do I need to take care of myself spiritually?
How do I need to take care of myself physically?
How do I need to take care of myself financially?
How do I need to take care of myself educationally?
How do I need to take care of myself emotionally?

**Be Me**

Speak my truth.
Voice my wants.
Be silent and alone.
Focus on health.
Aware of my presence.
Tune into my intuition.
Trust God's plan.
Complete my goals.
Let go of fears and worry.
Be loud and fun.
Take up space.
Connect with others.
Honor my needs.
Create my future.
Share my story.
Inspire others.

Dear Heart,

You waited for love when you were little, and it was always there. It's different from what you thought it should look like. You wanted presence and most of the time, the gift was in the absence. You didn't need to wait for love; it was there for everyone. All people wanted you. All wanted you to be happy. Everyone felt guilty about not giving you the love in the way that young you needed, but in reality, it was always there. You were never abandoned or lost. You were on the path that God planned for you. Your journey continues to develop you and to fulfill your purpose. You have been loved, are loved, and will be loved.

Love,
Love

**Love Allows**

Love allows.
Love allows another to take the burden from your shoulders.
Love allows you to be seen and heard.
Love allows another to share in the grief, sorrow, or pain.
To share in the overwhelm, fear, or exhaustion.
To share joy, happiness, and memories.
Love allows the connection of both heart and soul.
Love allows your heart to be held by another.
Love allows.

Dear Emilie,

Be yourself. Trust your intuition and your guidance from God. Believe the path you are on is the correct one. Your heart and soul will always guide you on the road that you're meant to be on. You know the road is going to come with potholes and curves and sometimes dead ends but you also have the ability to turn around and choose a different direction. You have navigated so much of life on your own. You need to believe that your ideas have value. What you want, wish for, and have dreams about is important not only to you, but to the world.

You, for your sake more than theirs, need to be the mom that you want your kids to witness. A woman who has suffered and comes out on the other side with healing and joy. A widow that can find love again. A person who follows their dreams and makes decisions based on their beliefs and their purpose. A mom who only wants a better life for her kids and a lifestyle that they do not feel abandoned or unwanted. When you do what you feel is right deep down inside and you forget to think about what others might say or feel, this allows your children to see that they, too, can make decisions based on what they want.

Everyone has the right to feel a certain way about a situation. You have a right to feel a certain way about a situation. These feelings might not match up, and somebody might feel hurt or upset, but they're not angry with you. If they're angry about the decision, then it's more about who they are and what paths they've followed than anything to do with the path that you are choosing. If you want something, then you should go for it. If you believe something is true, then you need to honor that truth. If your soul is speaking to you, you need to have trust that it will never misguide you. It doesn't mean that everything is going to come easily and that everything is going to be logical or easy to understand. Things might still be scary.

You know more than one thing can exist at a time. You can be nervously excited. You can be joyfully anxious. You can be lit up and exhausted at the same time. But if your heart says go and be this version of you right now, then that's who you need to be. It's your birthright to feel happy with the choices you're making. Your self-worth can never be changed. Your self-confidence can only grow stronger when you're making decisions.

You are loved by so many people, and that is never going to change, no matter what choices you make or the places you go, or the things you do. People may come and go from your life because you're not a match for them at the moment. Think back to all of the people who have been on or off your path. People you've traveled with for years and others that have only been there for a short time. Every person is on a different path on the same journey. Many times, our paths will cross each other, but the length of time will vary depending on when both people get what they need from the situation.

Focus on seeing your experiences as gifts from God. They were given to you to be able to help others. Your story is someone else's guide, and you can help many people even if your materials are not perfect in your eyes. Your story needs to be given to the world.

Raw is okay. Raw is believable. Raw is where others are. Be here. Be now. Be aware. Choose to see what's in front of you.

Choose to be with those around you. Changing the moment to feel your best. The past is gone, and you don't control the future.

God has always given you everything you need and will continue to do so. Live here now. Choose the moment. Tomorrow has enough worries of its own, so don't let them ruin today. The long-term picture lets you let go of fear. Just do the right thing now to prevent future problems. It's okay if you act differently or if people tease you. They need you. Speak your truth because you have the right to be happy, seen, and heard. Your desires matter.

Love,
Your Truth

**Restate**

I am worthy.
I am not abandoned.
I was never left alone.
I was cared for.
I am loved.
I am smart.
I am enough.
I love my mind, body, and soul.
I can grow and change.
I can share who I am.
I trust God and his plan and purpose.
I believe in love.

I can choose.
I can have wants.
I can have desires.
I speak my truth.
My needs are valid.
I deserve to feel joy.
I can want things others don't.
I can stop doing things I no longer want to.
I can decide.
I can change my mind.
I can put myself first.
I am worthy.
God made me worthy.
I am loved.
I am wanted.
I am never alone.
My choice matters.
I heard.
I am here now for a reason.
I am strong, smart, and beautiful.

Dear Emilie,

The emotion of love can be really confusing. I think everybody experiences love in a different way and expresses love in a different way, and it makes it really hard to know if you are truly loved.

You have always been loved by so many different people, and reflecting on how each of those persons loved you shows you how it really had nothing to do with who you were as a person all along.

Your mom loved you by teaching you to be independent and strong. Bruce loved you by staying away when he couldn't make you feel safe and secure. Your dad loved you by providing for you. Steve loved you by always wanting you to grow and become you. Your kids love you by wanting to still be with you even though they're not little anymore. Chris loves you by making you choose things and be happy.

Your parents loved you because you were created out of love. You gave them joy because of your personality. Steve loved you because of how you treated him and accepted him. Your kids love you because you offer them security and unconditional love. They know no matter what they do or say, you're going to always be there for them. Chris loves you because you show him a different way of living and loving. The students you worked with for all of those years loved you because you believed in them, and they knew you had their back and that you would do anything to help them learn and be okay. Your colleagues loved you because you were outgoing, kind, and compassionate.

You love hard. You love despite. You love because you can see all sides of a situation. You love because you were loved. You don't want anyone ever to feel unwanted, unsafe, unloved, abandoned, unworthy or broken. You want everyone to feel a part of your life and a connection to you. You cannot love somebody that you have not connected with. You cannot just tell somebody "I love you." Hearing people use that phrase casually bothers you because it should be reserved for a deep, heartfelt, strong connection with somebody. It has to be based on trust and commitment. Once you love someone, it's so hard for that love to be broken. Even when situations are confusing or difficult to understand, you can still see the love being given.

Remember when you were told that your heart was both a strength and a weakness? You knew exactly what that meant. You might not always make the best decisions based on a situation because you think with your heart first. You want people to feel okay and to be heard. You want everyone to be felt on a soul level. But not everybody has your heart. Not everybody can see good things in people or in situations. Not everyone has empathy or compassion for others. Some people focus on themselves and only on what's best for them. Some people have addictions or mental illnesses that don't allow them to care for, love, and support those around them. You must believe that your love is the greatest gift.

People feel comfortable with you because you can't help but offer them understanding or kindness. You can't help but care. You can't help but see the good. You can't not want others to be okay. You need others to experience being heard and knowing that their voice matters. And this is a good thing. Keep loving others. Keep sharing your experiences and stories so the world can heal in the same way you have, from experiences. Your heart and love are the biggest gifts you can give. Your understanding that your heart keeps growing new spaces to allow others to be a part of your love life is incredible. You being able to love multiple people who were raising you while loving your friends and being in love with two different men and three different children shows your purpose. God put you here to love deeply.

But you also need to accept the love. Even if somebody else's definition of love is different than yours or if they show it in a way that doesn't match how you think it should be. Allow people to love you by helping. Ask people for what you need. Allow people to honor your choices, wants, and needs. Allow others to do things for you without the need to reciprocate or pay. Allow others to hear your voice and your story.

Love,
Love

Dear Tired Emilie,

Rest is productive. It's not lazy, and it's not wasteful. You have permission to rest, do nothing, just breathe, relax, be honest, and enjoy stillness and silence. Sit and be still; no sound. Wear an eye mask, light a candle, feel the floor, and turn on the fireplace to listen to your soul and intuition. Trust what you are being told, and be present. Don't worry about the past or the future. You have the gift of reflection. See where you are today. Allow your mind, body, and soul to recover and reset. Put time in your schedule to be you. Choose your desires. Be who you want to be. Focus on your needs. Take time to be still, in the darkness, and feel the feelings.

Light your own lamp first. Allow others to care for you if you need it. You don't have to be everyone to be a caretaker.

Stillness is a gift so you can feel and hear the vibrations of love at all levels of your soul and all levels of your being of the past, present, and future; the feelings of love, sorrow, grief, pain, healing, joy, elation, fear, and safety. Be silent. Lie down to feel the energy in every ounce of your being, to know the energy shifts and that they can be replaced with new understanding and acceptance as to why it is there and the purpose. Connect with all the musicians of your soul to hear the different voices that create you as an incredible being.

Love,
Stillness

**Let Me Be**

I don't want to be anyone right now.
I want to just be me.
I want to look ahead and see the choices I have.
I want to pick one of them
I want to do it for just a couple of minutes.
Then I'll change my mind and pick something else.
No one is going to stop me.
No one is going to tell me my choice is wrong.
My decision makes me feel happy.

I might choose to run down the beach.
I might choose to lay in the sand.
I might choose to throw rocks.
I might choose to take a nap.
I might choose to sit and pray.
I might choose to find agates.
I might choose to build a fort.
I might choose to go for a swim.
I might choose to take pictures.
I might choose to watch the raven.
I might choose to listen to the fog horn.
I might choose to scream and yell.
I might choose to simply breathe.
I might choose to be me.
I might choose.

---

*What does rest say to you if you gave it a voice?*

Dear You,

Use reflection. Go back and see the wins, the successes, the things that brought you joy and made you smile. That's who you are now. Do more of those things. Focus on what's going well, that's lighting you up; the positives outweigh the negatives. Even things that seemed horrible and tragic gave you lessons. Now, share those with others.

Not all is sunshine and roses, but it's a cloudy day and some roses have thorns. Focus on the teeny bit of sunlight shining in a newly opened bloom. It's your choice to go down a path and enjoy the journey, even though there are hardships like death, anger, misunderstanding, and lack of maturity, and see the love, kindness, protection, and lessons. See the joy, be grateful, live with love, teach purposefully, and create with your heart.

Speak about your feelings and thoughts without fearing how they will affect others. Scream when you need to be loud. Share your stories. Be your voice. Focus on the positive experiences and see that the choices others made affected your feelings about yourself. See the love that everyone had for you when they could give you love. Not everyone has the capacity for love all of the time.

It was never about you. Remove the facade, take off the mask, and uncover the truth. You are never alone. You don't have to do it all. You can and should get help. Be true. Allow yourself to be loved and helped by others.

Looking back, don't just see the confusion and the mess. Look back and see the love, the kindness, the moments of worthiness, and the times you mattered. You have permission to forget the negative, the hurt, the abandonment, the self-doubt, the feelings of unworthiness. See your life as a place where you grew, that you were loved, smart, and strong. See the growth into who you are today and know there'll be more growth tomorrow and in the future.

You are always the best version of yourself, no matter what you are doing or feeling. You can only do what you know. Keep learning. Keep changing as the circumstances change. Always love yourself. Always move forward. Stay in the present moment. Throw worry about the future out the window. Throw fear of the future off the roof. Trust yourself and God's plan for you. Even when times have been hard and awful, it turned out that you were able to see the peace and the joy, and eventually the purpose.

Love,
Your Heart

**Here**

I let go of my past with forgiveness and love.
I let go of my future with trust and openness.
I am here
I am present.

The layers I've built and collected crumble away
The me I've always been is revealed
Loved, wanted, cared for, worthy, and valuable

See me
Hear me
Know me
I am here

I have always been here

**What if...**

if it goes well?
no one is upset?
I'm right?
I feel like me?
if someone is hurt?
someone gets upset?
someone leaves me?
I feel worse?
I feel guilty?
I feel confused?
I feel unworthy?
I don't deserve this?
this makes me look bad?
this makes me love less?
I don't know?

no one actually cares?
no one gets upset?
no one leaves?
I feel better?
I feel loved?
I feel affirmed?
I feel worthy?
I do deserve it all?
this makes me feel good?
this makes me feel loved more?
I do know?

---

*Answer the question "what if?".*

Dear Entrepreneur,

Accept money with gratitude. Feel joy when getting paid for a service you provide. Collaborating with others allows people to learn and help themselves. You are helping, but your experience and expertise are also valuable. See money as energy. It grows as you accept it. It doesn't grow on trees, but it does grow when you're ready to receive it with love and gratitude. Be grateful for those who have supported you while allowing you to teach and earn money. Release the fear and see the gift of collaboration with others and the gift of sharing your gifts with others— charge for your time, talent, expertise, and effort. Accept money as a form of gratitude. Allow others to thank you for giving of yourself.

Relax enough to collaborate with others and to share your gifts. The exchange of money is an endless cycle of giving and receiving; they give and receive. Money works like a bridge. It travels both to and from you for your services, your bills, your wants, and your needs. Making money does not have to be dark or filled with self-doubt. Your time has value. The experiences you've had have value.

Money has value. Understand that when you give someone cash or transfer funds, you are thanking them for letting you have access to their gifts, skills, and talents, and it works the other way just as easily. When you share something about what you've learned and what you've experienced, that's helping somebody else on their journey. Think of yourself as a cab driver. You have these experiences that other people want to experience as well, and they will come along for the ride and pay you to be part of their journey. You must put yourself out there and be available so others can get the ride they need.

Teach others. Love others. Build connections. Trust. Live your purpose. You are the one who inspires and influences others because sharing your story allows others to be felt, seen, and heard.

Love,
Your Purpose

## Deserving

I am deserving.
I have a story to share.
I deserve happiness.
I am proud of my business.
I honor the different parts of me.
I experience joy and connection.
I love helping others.
I have self-respect.
I honor my needs.
I am proud of myself.
I am deserving.

---

*What are you saying about money?*
*How do you feel about money?*
*What are your finances saying to you?*
*How would you like to feel about money?*

Dear Emilie,

Be you. Be happy. Be loved. Be supported. He'll tell you if something is not right or if it's too much. He has the right to set boundaries as well. Always be you. You don't need to put up a curtain that blocks the real you. Let the trust flow so that you'll both be able to set boundaries, even if they differ. Come out and see what you really desire. Tell him what you want, what feels good, what is a turn-on and what is a turn-off. Ask, speak up, share, and offer based on your wants and desires.

You are a sexual being and have the right to be loved as such. Go within, reflect, learn, and notice what you enjoy. Give yourself the gift of self-love and self-confidence in all situations. Speak your truth, speak your wishes and dreams. Choose you and choose your pleasure. Love every part of who you are and share that with the world. Be you in all situations. Choose your reality. Choose what to share without defeating your wants and interests. Honor your sexuality. Love yourself. Trust yourself.

You have the freedom to do and say what your heart wants. Leave the worries and fears behind. Focus on the present moment. Trust that you are loved unconditionally. Trust what you've wanted in the past. What was an easy 'yes' before? What happened before when you trusted your voice? Trust your instincts. Trust what makes you feel good. You may have things similar to your past, or that seem scary, but put yourself first. Do not worry about others' thoughts or possible judgments. He loves you. He can say yes or no, just like you do. Communicate what you want. Share what makes you feel passionate. Allow your body to let go and feel pleasure. Be loud. Use your voice. Let him see the raw you. Know that what happens in your body is a part of who you have always been. Reflect on what has made you feel beautiful and sexy in the past. Dream about what your relationship with your body can be now.

Love,
Your Sexuality

## Who Am I

a loving partner
a loving parent
an agate picker
a beachgoer
an author
a writer
a poet
a cook
a cleaner
a homeowner
one who reads
one who creates
one who feels
a business owner
a retired teacher
a photographer
a grief guide
a journal mentor

Dear Emilie,

I want you to know that food is just a tool. It's a way to provide me with energy. None of it is wrong, and none of it is more right than another kind, but you have to listen to me to know what it needs and when. There are days when you are going to need more sugar or fats or carbohydrates or protein or vitamins. Each of these serves a different purpose, and you get to choose what you want to focus on, mix and match, or avoid because you are in control of this part of your life.

This factor in your life is a necessity. You know that you must eat. You can make decisions now that have nothing to do with the decisions you've made in the past. You feel like you have made bad or wrong choices because of how I look. You have made choices a lot of times around food because you were living in survival mode. It was necessary for you to stop taking time to meal plan, purchase groceries, and make food for multiple people every day. You had many other things to focus on, and that's okay.

You can choose day by day what is going to feel good for me. What is going to make your mind happy? What is going to be pleasing to your soul? What you need to do for the other areas of your life: time and money and patience and energy. Your children know what healthy foods are. They understand how to make recipes and get the food they need for their bodies.

Thinking back, how much of your life revolves around food? So many of the memories you have of growing up, celebrating, and being congratulated are all focused on food. Your memories of breakfasts with your grandparents in the recipes that your mom and dad made, and things that Bruce made for you, birthday celebrations, graduation parties, babies, bridal showers, and all of those things related to food. You don't know how to celebrate things without having food.

Choose what makes me feel the best.

Love,
Your Body

## Foods to Celebrate

Everything was based on food
Memories of breakfast on a yellow plate
Recipes passed down for breakfast foods
Jam made after berries were picked
Family meals together
Special treats for birthday parties
Peanut butter balls and cookies for Christmas
Fruit cup and plum pudding for Thanksgiving
Cakes or pies to celebrate a birthday
Hors d'oeuvres served for Christmas Eve
Everyone brings something to celebrate the new year
Gatherings with food celebrating babies and weddings
Burnt cinnamon rolls on Christmas morning

Do we know how to celebrate without having food?
Could we just get together and celebrate our worth?
Should people only gather to share good news and best wishes?
Gifts could be given without sharing a meal
People get together because of who we are, not what we bring

Love isn't about the way our stomachs feel
Love is about how our hearts feel

---

*If your body could speak, what do you think it would say?*

Em,

I'm upset with myself because I never wanted you to feel like you had to make all of the money and financial decisions on your own. I always wanted to be a team with that. I wanted it to go a certain way, and I know that you had a different upbringing. I wish we had had more conversations about what our money story was, and how we were going to create a money story that worked for both of us. I wish I would have been more questioning, not because I doubted you but because I should have also been aware of what was going on and not making you feel alone.

I know you are smart. I know you have the math skills and the brains to figure out money budgeting, and finance. You do an incredible job running this house, buying almost everything we need, organizing vacations, camping, parties, Christmas, and everything else that requires a lot of financial planning. My trust in you is not broken because we have credit card debt, or because you were borrowing money that we didn't have.

We will get out of this. We are still better off than so many people. You understand what you were doing, and that's half the battle to us creating something different. I don't want you to be laying in bed every night feeling like you're going to throw up out of fear that I will find out the balance of our credit card. I don't want you worried that I'm going to be mad or that I'm going to want to leave you because of a money decision that I was part of. I wish you believed in yourself enough to tell me that we were struggling. I wish you knew it wasn't your fault. I want you to feel like you can tell me absolutely anything, and you know that I'm going to always love you. I wish instead of panicking about what could happen in the future, that you went back and remembered what's already happened in the past. Reflect on the times we've gone through were real challenges, and it's been okay. Keep in mind that we have argued over some things, and we've been okay. There have been a few times that you and I have failed together, and we've been okay.

I have never stopped loving you, no matter what you have said or done. I want to work through this together. I want to figure out how we can have what we want while also saving for the future and being prepared for when we need to do a car repair, buy new tires, or fix the refrigerator or those things that are going to happen. I want us to be able to go on vacations, go camping, and do things with the kids. I don't like either of us lying in bed trying to figure out how we're going to buy groceries. We make enough that we should not be living paycheck to paycheck. We should have enough in our savings to cover different expenses that will come up and not go into debt when a holiday comes up, or an emergency happens.

I love being able to support the parish and buy stuff from the millions of fundraisers that we participate in because of our kids or the students at school. I like knowing that if you and I want to go out to dinner or take a trip out of town, we have the money to pay for a hotel for a night or two without rearranging everything. I want you to be happy with the decisions we make and the budget we create and I think we're on the same page as far as our dreams for the future.

Love,
Steve

**Partnership**

I will always be your partner
I will be together with you
I want to share your joy and happiness
I want to share your worries and fears
I want to share my joy and happiness
I want to share my worries and fears
I want to work together to make our house a home
I want to work together to keep our marriage strong
I want to work together to be the best parents we can be
I want to take vacations and spend time alone
I want to work on finances and budgeting
I want to work on dreams and hopes for our future
I want to help the boys become independent
I want to gather with both of our families
I want to celebrate holidays and birthdays together
I want to be partners on the next steps in our journey
I want to be empty nesters together
I want to celebrate our 25th and 50th anniversaries with you
I will always love you
I will always be your partner

Emilie,

Just tell him! Just get it over with and tell him what you're thinking, what you're worried about, and how much money you don't have. It is not healthy for you to panic every time the phone rings for fear that the credit card company is going to call and he's going to hear the balance and know that you haven't paid it off every month. Being able to share your finances with him is something that you've been able to do since day one. You talked about money, what you wanted money to go for and how it was going to work.

You are not a failure because the system you have isn't working. You are not stupid because you can't figure out how to cover extra expenses that are coming up when the savings aren't there. Your financial statements are not a reflection of who you are as a person, or how you are as a wife, or how you are as a mom. You are doing the absolute best you can and you're doing it mostly independently.

Don't be afraid to ask for help. Finances are one of the hardest things that people have to figure out and go through, and you didn't have a lot of financial discussions when you were little. You didn't know how much the bills were or even what the bills being paid were or about property taxes. You didn't know that putting money on a credit card and not being able to pay it off had 30% interest on everything that was on that card. You knew that when you went shopping and there were a bunch of things on sale and everything was a good deal that you just put it in your cart and you brought it home. You never worried where the money came from to pay for those things. You can only do something different when you learn something different.

Talk to him. Tell him what you're thinking. Tell him what you're scared of. Tell him you're worried and concerned about paying for things and buying different things. Share with him your dreams of being able to take vacations and to go traveling and to attend retreats. Let him share with you his thoughts on how a budget should work. You're both very smart when it comes to numbers.

You've got this, but you need to work together. You can't keep trying to do all of this on your own. You are not Superwoman. You are not alone on this journey. You have a husband that loves you and wants to support you and has always been there for you. He can't help you with something he doesn't know you're struggling with. He doesn't read your journals to see your panic over the bills each month. He doesn't see that you're a people-pleaser to the point that you will put your health at risk to make sure that everybody is happy and that everybody gets what they want. Your kids are also intelligent and will understand if finances change and things happen differently in the household, they are happy to eat at home as a family and they don't care if the food is made at home or if it's bought from a store or if it's picked up in a drive-thru. Your kids are happy to play games and don't need something new for whatever electronic system they have. Your kids love to spend time camping and out at the camp.

Everyone is going to be okay if you tell them what's going on, because there's a solution and you're not going to find it trying what you have been. You need to do something new and you need to do something soon. He will be less upset if he finds out now than if you wait for another five months, six months, or two years and then finds out that this has been happening for so long.

Just because you think he's going to be mad or angry with you doesn't mean that he doesn't still love you. He's not going to leave you over this. You know that. You know you've worked out everything before. You know he supports you 100%. He's probably going to blame himself.

You've got other people in your life too, that will help with this. Your dad is good with money. His dad is good with money and helped so many people with loans when he owned the collection agency. It's going to all work out.

Think about how you'll feel knowing that you can pay your bills, put money in savings, and do fun things without being nauseated or unable to sleep. Think about how you'll feel not having the weight of all of this on your shoulders alone. Think about how much stronger your marriage is going to be if you're able to work on this together instead of it all being your job. You have taken it on, and you have done well. You know so much about prices and shopping and values and deals. You've got this. Even if you want to continue running the house's finances, he will let you. He doesn't want to do it. He thinks you enjoy it. He thinks you're doing a great job at it. He believes in you and that you're always going to do what's best for the family because that's the person he loves. Tell him today!

Love,
Your Soul

## Who's in Control

Do you control money, or does it control you?
Do you tell money where to go, or does it decide?
When you receive money, do you practice gratitude?
Are you only experiencing a feeling of relief?
Do you have money to do what you want?
Is abundance just a dream?
Do you feel gratitude about accepting money?
Are you worried you're charging too much
Do you fear the other person doesn't have it?

You are the one who controls money.
You decide how it's spent.
You decide how it's earned.
You determine where it comes from and where it goes.
You experience gratitude when you receive money
You have enough to pay bills and unexpected expenses.
You have the money to follow your dreams.
Your time and talent have value.
People who need the service have the funds available.

Dear Emilie,

I will love you no matter what version of you you are living in.

If you want to go back to work and work at night, I will love you. If you want to move to an apartment on your own I will love you. If you want to travel the world, I will love you. If you start making decisions and speaking up for yourself, I will love you. If you decide to make your boys independent and pay for everything on their own, I will love you. If you choose not to attend a family event, I will love you. If you decide you want two or three days a week where you have no commitments with anybody but yourself, I will love you. If you decide to go on a retreat every month, I will love you. If you start believing in yourself and change your physical appearance, I will love you. If you decide to eat protein and vegetables at every meal, I will love you. If you shave your head and cover your body with tattoos, I will love you. If you swim in the ocean and lose your arm to a shark, I will love you. If you go off and do things by yourself because it makes you feel good, I will love you. If you stop doing the things you're doing now and do different things because it lights you up, I will love you. If you decide something in the morning and change your mind that night, I will love you. If you jump in the car and drive somewhere to be alone, I will love you. If you spend your money the way you want on yourself, I will love you. If you tell me what you want for dinner, I will love you. If you change the type of clothes you're wearing, I will love you. If you decide to stay up until 2:00 in the morning and sleep till noon, I will love you.

Your heart will always love everyone around you and want what's best for them, and as you learn to love yourself and want what's best for you, I will love you. The deep parts of you will never change. And because of that, my love for you will never change.

Love,
Everyone

**What I've Been Told**

So many people have told me:
You were wanted
You were loved
You are beautiful
You are talented
You have a big heart
You're a great wife
You're a great mom
You're a great teacher.
You should be a lector.
You should go to church every week.
You should follow the rules of society.
Don't be too spiritual.

But what about the story that I told myself?
You were given up.
You were abandoned.
You are fat.
You're too loud.
You're not brave.
You're only wanted because it's comfortable.
You're not worthy.
You can't trust people to stick around.
You can't charge people money for teaching them.
You can't be your true self around everyone.
You'll grieve for so long.
You have to be everything for others before yourself.

What my soul says
You are enough!
You are worthy!
You are loved!
You need to be you!

Dear World,

Why did I start Calm Water Writing? Why do I create things to share with other people? Why do I spend parts of my days making workbooks, writing books, offering workshops, creating Facebook events, booking retreats, and finding places to hold workshops? Why do I offer one-on-one sessions for bullet journaling, self-care journaling, and help with healing from grief? Why do I record a podcast? Why have I kept a blog for so many years? Why did I launch a website?

It's all because I want to help other people. I have gone through a lot in my life. I have dealt with so many different emotions and realize how many of those emotions go together and can switch back and forth within a day, sometimes minute to minute. Through writing, journaling, and other activities like coloring, I spend time by the water and SoulCollage®, connecting with many parts of my soul. I want that for other people. I believe that God gave me my soul the minute I was conceived. He had a purpose for me. He knew who I was going to be, the journey I was going to take, and the experiences I was going to have, and he gave me all the parts I needed to be able to live through each of those pieces. Little bits of who I am were needed for every one of those moments of my life.

The biggest piece of my soul is empathy. To me, empathy is being able to feel love for somebody because of what they're going through because I've gone through something similar. None of us have the exact same experiences, even if the situations are similar. We all go through childhood differently. We all have different ways of being in a relationship with our parents, our siblings, our partners, or our children. We all had different versions of being students in school. We all feel love in various ways and, therefore, give it in other ways and receive it differently. We all have different needs regarding our physical bodies, including what we need to eat and drink and how we have to move, sleep, and rest. We are each on our own spiritual path, and whether you're connected to God or another higher power or the universe, you still understand that there's more than just you.

Writing and journaling are things that every person can do as a way to document feelings and experiences. It's a way to process what's happening. It's a way of connecting with the different parts of your soul and how each of those pieces interacts with what's happening around you. You can go back and reflect on times from when you were still inside your mother's womb, through your childhood, after school, and through relationships. Writing helps with processing how you learn and how you see the world, as well as how you take in information and share your thoughts and ideas. By doing this, you are able to look into the future and think about the dreams you have and the goals you want to achieve, the places you want to go, the person you want to be remembered as being, and the influence you want to have on the world. Thinking through the worries and fears and confusion that you have, all while trusting that your purpose is being lived out and the experiences you're having are the ones that you're meant to have, can be a part of journaling. I want to share my experiences with grief and joy and abandonment and love and struggles and success and hard work and relaxation and planning and relief and intuition and understanding. So many emotions go together at the same time.

Journaling is the way I speak to myself. It's the way I speak to the world. It's the way I was made to communicate. It's the way my soul speaks. Journaling takes on so many different forms in my life, whether it's a brain dump before I go to bed so that my thoughts can be on paper instead of bouncing around inside my mind, or writing down little images of the things I did throughout the day that brought me joy as a form of self-care, or making a list of the prayers and miracles that I've experienced. Or going back on reflecting on amazing memories I have of my grandma making me French toast on a yellow plate at the camp. Or writing through the tears while I think of all the things I won't get to experience with Steve. Or responding to journal prompts from a business coach or words

I've received from emotion code messages or lyrics to a song that keeps coming on the radio or my playlist. Sometimes, it's short, and it only takes me a couple of minutes to get my thoughts out, and I feel better. Other times, I have to write the same thoughts and ideas over and over while different little teeny tiny pieces pop up, and the realization comes after many, many times. Sometimes, it's on paper, which is the most therapeutic, and sometimes, it's just voiced into my phone. Sometimes, it's on scrap paper with a sketchy pencil, and other times it's on beautiful paper in an amazing notebook with an incredibly smooth black pen. My soul needs a voice, and journaling is where I get to hear it.

Love,
Emilie

**My experiences might help you...**

heal
learn
not feel alone
not feel weird
find hope
find joy
believe in yourself
see your journey
learn to write
learn to feel
connect with others
create a practice
deepen self-love
follow your dreams

Steve,

When you look down on me or hang around on the porch and watch me live this life, I want you to be happy with the version of me that's active now. I don't want you to be upset that I wasn't this version of me when you were alive. I'm sorry I wasn't healing the little versions of myself. I'm sorry I didn't feel worthy of being loved. I'm sorry I constantly filled the calendar so that I didn't have time to focus on my emotions and feelings. I'm sorry that I didn't let you in fully. I'm sorry that I didn't trust myself enough to be angry, to get upset, and to express the pain I was feeling. I'm sorry that my feelings of unworthiness didn't allow me to be me fully. I'm sorry that you only get to see this version of me from heaven.

I wish I had known different things when we first met in high school and throughout our marriage. I wish I had understood different things when figuring out how to be parents. I wish I had felt confident to share my wants and needs without feeling guilty for putting myself first. I was so afraid that if I took time to figure out what I wanted, you would be angry and that if you got angry, you would leave. I see now that that was ridiculous. I understand that your love didn't work that way. I know that you tried to get me to make decisions and to do what I wanted to do.

Thank you for always loving me and encouraging me and being there for me. I will always hold a space in my heart for you. I pray you never stop watching over me no matter what version of me I'm being.

Love,
Me (6 years later)

**It's Hard**

It's hard to let go
It's hard to move forward

They are not forgotten
They are not loved less
They are not left behind
They are still in my heart
They are a part of me

It's hard to feel joy when there's anger
It's hard to feel okay when you're not
It's hard to smile through the tears
It's okay to grieve the loss
It's okay to focus on the memories
It's okay to feel and focus on love

Grief and joy coexist

Chris,

I'm afraid to tell you who I am and the things that run through both my brain, and my heart on a daily basis. I'm afraid that if you could understand how unworthy and unconfident I feel a lot of the time, then it would make you angry. And I fear that if people get angry, they leave. I don't want you to leave. So I let you make decisions. I let you choose what we do, where we go, and how we spend our time. We have so many things that we like to do that I know you'll pick something that I'm okay with.

I'm working hard on figuring out what I like to do and what brings me joy. I'm working on making myself happy. I'm learning that I can put myself first and that others won't get upset by that.

I'm scared to have conversations with you because I often share things through writing, and so talking through this is going to be hard. But I trust you. I love you. I want you to know the version of me that I'm trying to be, so you can determine if this way of being is someone you can also be in love with. I think that can happen. I think it's just another layer of the woman you've fallen in love with. I think it's always been there but hidden, and now I'm pulling back the covers. I think you're going to like her better. I think you're going to understand her more.

Thank you for always dealing with my crazies and listening to my ramblings and weird thoughts. Thank you for making me share through talking, not just writing.

Love,
Me (4 years in)

**Chris' Song**

I've grown through my love for you.
I've grown into a person who can make some decisions
even if it is as simple as what to eat.
I've grown to believe that I can be loved and wanted by another human.
I've grown to believe that God brings us the people in our lives
when it's meant to be and not a moment sooner.
I've grown in my enjoyment of nature by seeing waterfalls
and watching sunsets and searching for copper.
I've grown as a person to become more independent
in the choices I make based on what I need and what I want.
I've grown to understand that my past has turned me into the person
that you fell in love with.
I've grown to be myself around you, even when I might be a little crazy
or a little loud or talk a little too much.
I've grown to look forward to Sunday morning breakfasts
of pancakes and bacon.
I've grown to be grateful for the teeny little things
like having you start my car, make me tea, or leave a banana.
I've grown through my love for you.

———————————————

*What are you afraid to say to someone you love?*
*What do you fear someone would say to you if you told them what you really feel?*

Dear Healers,

I think I need to take a step back. I think I need to do it. Take the leap, use the different tools you have given me, the skills you've taught me, and the lessons I've learned, and do it on my own. I think I need to put time into my schedule to be alone, still, meditate, reflect, hope, and dream. To just be with me. To connect with all the parts of my soul and my mind and my body and my spirit on my own. But I'm afraid. What if I do it wrong? What if I don't know how? What if there's no right way, and that's supposed to be okay? I want there to be a right way. I want to know what that is. What if I have the answers, but because I've never tried to find them on my own it's just scary because of it being unknown and new? What if everything I've done has just brought me to this place?

In one of my coaching sessions it was brought up that I always want my coach to get something out of the session as well and that's true. I don't want to be a burden. I don't want it to feel like a waste of time or that I didn't do what I was supposed to do. Or that I got too emotional or too deep or went off track. And yet, the other part of me knows that it is time that's supposed to be for me and that I can go and do and say whatever I need to. This is something that I have paid for and made time for, but there's also a bit of myself that I always hold back. There's always a little bit of fear. There's always worry about judgment and a concern that you're going to get angry or upset. I don't want anyone to be angry. If you get angry then you'll leave. You'll leave because I'm not worthy. If I share the true me and what I'm actually feeling and I share my anger and frustrations, it will be upsetting. I don't even know how to express that I'm angry, frustrated, and confused. Those aren't emotions that I like to feel in my body. I don't like the tightness in my chest, the headache that it brings on and the tears that come and the pressure in my eyes, and the constriction in my throat. I don't want people to see that version of me.

I need to find a way to feel all the emotions on my own in a safe place. I need to be angry. I need to yell, scream, throw things, and hit things. I need to write angry letters. I need to swear and say things that might be hurtful to all kinds of people from my past.

And I need to do forgiveness work. Forgiveness to myself and to so many others for the anger and the judgment and the negative feelings I have had when everyone was only doing the best they could with what they had in the situations they were in.

So thank you for the love, the support and the honesty you have provided. Thank you for the allowance of vulnerability and the different layers and versions of who I am to be visible and witnessed.

Love,
Emilie

## Soulful Menu

joyful mornings
peaceful weekends
rejuvenating water
compelling stories
informational podcast
clean house
responsible finances
restful sleep
lengthy drives
powerful journaling
dynamic photos
home cooked meals
trusting faith
focused activities
shared hobbies
loving friendships
creative projects
collaborative retreats
relaxing evenings
healthy movement
nutritional snacks
meaningful connections
productive planning
believing intuition
various genres
fun games
beautiful family
soulful women
guided spirit
soul collage
grief movement
healing sessions
faithful practices

Anger!

I AM SICK AND TIRED OF BEING ANGRY BUT NEVER SHOWING IT! I AM SICK AND TIRED OF FEELING UNWORTHY AND FEELING UNWANTED! I AM FED UP! I AM DONE! I AM OVER IT! I AM READY TO BE ME! TO KNOW WHAT I WANT! TO FIGURE OUT MY DESIRES! TO SPEAK MY TRUTH AND TO BE HEARD! I AM DONE TRYING TO BE EVERYTHING FOR EVERYONE ALL THE TIME! I AM DONE PUTTING EVERYONE BEFORE ME! I AM DONE FEELING LEFT BEHIND.

I am getting off the steps and moving out into the world to do the things I want to do and have always wanted to do, but I felt like if I did them, I would make others upset or feel abandoned. I never want anyone to feel hurt or to get upset, especially with me. If you get upset, then you might leave, and I cannot handle anyone else leaving me.

I AM WORTHY! I HAVE THE RIGHT TO BE HAPPY! I AM ABLE TO CHOOSE THINGS THAT MAKE ME SMILE, MAKE ME EXPERIENCE JOY, AND LIGHT ME UP!

I am not sure what those things even are, because I have pushed them down for so long to make sure that everyone around me is okay and happy; I'm going to figure it out. I am going to try little things first and then bigger things, and I am going to try not to think about others so much. I don't ever want to hurt someone on purpose. That won't change. That is who I am at my core. I always want others to be happy, but it can no longer be at my expense. I also deserve to be happy. I deserve to get to do things I want to experience, things that are fun and joyful. I should not have to do things I hate because it might upset someone if I ask for them to be done or pay someone to do them. I have the right to spend my money how I wish. I have the right to spend my time how I wish. I have the right to use my mind and body in ways that bring me pleasure.

Love,
Deep Inside

## Hey Anger!

I see you.
I feel you.
I want you.
I need you.

I know you are there.
I know you exist.
I know you hurt.
I know you suffer.

You are allowed to be expressed.
You should not be caged up.
You will not be silenced.
You should not be pent up.

Come out.
Let me hear you.
It's okay.
You'll be alright.

Let yourself go.
Let yourself out.
Let me experience you.
Let others know you.

You are valid.
You are meant to be here.
You are important.
You matter in my life.

Scream.
Yell.
Swear.
Growl.

Be loud.
Be fierce.
Be scary.
Be alive.

---

*Where does your body feel and express anger?*
*Who needs to hear your anger and frustration?*

God!

I'm angry! I'm confused! I'm upset! I do not understand and have absolutely no idea why you thought it was a great idea to take Steve when you did. I don't know why you thought taking him while we were doing well and only twenty years into our marriage was a good time. I don't know why you thought 17, 15, and 11 were good ages for boys to deal with the death of a father. I don't know why, but while I was dealing with a lot at work, I then needed to learn how to be a widow and a single parent, too. I don't know why you thought I was strong enough to handle everything.

I also don't think it's fair that you let scumbags and people that do awful things stay on earth, and you take somebody who is a fantastic person who wants nothing more than to help everybody. It doesn't make any sense!

I know we're just supposed to trust everything that you do. That you have some miraculous plan all figured out, and we're supposed to just somehow believe that everything is going to work out and everybody's going to be okay, but it sucks! I don't like this feeling of being alone. I don't like having to teach my kids about grief and sorrow and anger and pain. Everybody goes through it, and life's not all peachy and great. I know we've got family and support and love and faith, and I know we've gotten through death before, and I know we're going to be fine. But it still hurts! And it's still awful. It is still confusing. I just don't want to get out of bed today. I don't want to face anybody else. I don't want people to see this side of my faith. I don't want people to see that I'm angry with you or questioning you.

I am mad at you! I am so angry at the things that I don't get to do with Steve and that he doesn't get to do with the boys. I'm so mad that his family and friends are going through this. I am so angry that I have to make decisions, and I don't like making decisions. I don't even know how to do a lot of the things that I'm now having to do. Why are you forcing me to do all of this!?! Will I ever understand? Will I ever know the purpose of this? Do I have to wait until I get to heaven to see why all this is happening? Will you give me signs that this is what was meant to be and this wasn't a mistake?

I'm grateful to whoever told me to be angry with you and that you could handle it. I hope it's true.

Amen

**ANGER**

LOUD but silent in my chest
HURT but also keeps me safe
BANG inside my head
FISTS made without contact
POUNDING of my heart in my chest
THROWING of objects to ease the pain
PAIN from the loss and grief
SORROW and sadness
LOSS and finality sets in
PENT UP and bottled up
TIGHTNESS in my body
SCARY because it's uncontrolled
UNKNOWN and new to me

*Express your anger or confusion to a higher power if needed.*

Dear Worrier,

Yes, I still want you to be around even when you're not feeling in the best mood. Even when you don't really know what you want to do today. When you're not feeling great, but you don't really know what's wrong. For example, you don't have a headache or an upset stomach, and you don't have a fever or diarrhea, but you just feel off. If all you want to do is lay around in your pajamas and watch movies that you've seen a million times, I still want you to be around. It's okay for you to have off days. It's okay for you to rest. You don't always have to be productive. Your body knows when you need to take a break. You don't always have to show up and go places and provide for others. You can do what you need to do to take care of yourself. I love you even if you haven't taken a shower. I love you when your hair is a mess. I love you when you don't know what to have for dinner, and ice cream is the only thing that sounds good.

Love,
Me

**Letters to Me**

Grab a paper, grab a pen, and write a letter to me
Tell me what you're feeling and what you want to say
Let the world hear your voice and your story
Know that your words are important and that they matter
Think about situations you've gone through
Reflect on happy and joyous times
Remember moments you felt successful and proud
Allow the feelings of love and worthiness to come through
Choose your words carefully
You are speaking to somebody very important
What you say and how you say it affects what you hear
Speak kindly to yourself
Offer words of encouragement
Give a voice to your emotions
Grant permission to speak your truth

Dear Fixer,

You were never meant to have to fix everything. It was not your job to keep relationships together. It was not your role to make sure that everyone was happy. You were not supposed to ensure that no one argued, got upset, was angry, or left. You were put here to be you. You were put here to be kind and compassionate and to have empathy. You were put here to be able to see all sides of a situation. You were put here to understand that everyone has different wants, needs, and desires. You were always meant to be a teacher.

From when you were very tiny, you played with stuffed animals and taught them how to do math, spelling, and to write their names. You convinced your friends to be students. You got excited when you got textbooks from the school. You knew all throughout school that you were going to be a teacher and that you were going to work with kids. It was not a surprise that your job growing up was to be a babysitter.

Choosing special education meant that you got to really build connections with the people and students you worked with, more so than other types of teaching. But you were still never meant to fix anyone. You were meant to teach. You were meant to provide the kids with tools so they could figure things out. You could not fix the homes they lived in, the parents they lived with, the mental health conditions or the learning disabilities. You could only provide support. You could only give them ideas. You could only share things that worked for you or that you had seen work for other people. It was then up to them to use them or not. You could build a connection with them. You could listen. You could love them. But you couldn't fix them because they weren't broken. Every situation and experience they had, taught them something. Every person they met and feeling they had was meant to be; even when it was hard, even when it seemed unfair or was wrong.

As your role now as a guide and healer you cannot fix anyone. You can only provide tools and ideas. You can give people things but they have to do the work themselves. They have to take the tools and use them in a way that's best for them.

You are also not broken. You cannot be fixed. No one can fix you. You can gather all of the tools from everyone around you but you have to then use the tools to live life. To process the emotions and feelings. To work with and love others. To interact with the world. To give and receive money. To teach workshops and share your knowledge. To honor the past and prepare for the future. To be present. To create a healthy body, mind and spirit. To honor the purpose that God gave you. And when you do that for you, then and only then will you be able to do the same for others.

Love,
The Teacher

## Who Have I Trained to Be?

A daughter
A granddaughter
A sister
A student
A friend
A swimmer
A girlfriend
A wife
A teacher
A daughter-in-law
A mom
A person of faith
A homemaker
A colleague
A writer
An author
A widow
A partner
A mother-in-law
An auntie
A business owner

But what about me?
Have I trained to be me?
Who offers that course?

---

What does your purpose tell you about who you are?

Dear Suit of Defense,

I know I put you on a lot. If people see who I am and see that I have wants and desires, they might get upset. And I wear you so I fit in better. I feel like I'm a part of the group or that I'm connected more closely with the person I'm with. I don't want to be seen as different or weird. I like situations to be calm and peaceful; when they're not, I feel guilty that I've done something wrong. I worry that someone will get mad or be angry with me. If people get angry, they'll leave, and I don't want to be left behind. I want to be included. So I'll continue to wear you so that others get to be themselves. It doesn't matter if inside I'm hurting or confused or angry. It only matters if the other people feel good and are happy. It doesn't matter if later I'll be upset and numb out. It doesn't matter if I don't sleep well. It just matters that everyone else is okay. Putting you on keeps the peace.

But I'm starting to take you off. I'm going to start small. I'm going to start with people I know are safe. I've started doing it a little bit more often and it feels okay. When I've done it, no one has gotten angry. I've spoken my truth a couple of times. I've made decisions about what I want to eat or where I want to go. A couple of times I've even asked for what I want to do.

I'm listening to my body, how it feels, and what it needs. Some days, it just needs to be home and rest. I just need to watch movies and be relaxed. I don't always have to be productive.

I'm feeling into what deciding based on my wants and needs feels like. I am starting to understand and believe that the uneasy feeling I have about how they will react is because of how long I've done that, but it doesn't have to be that way. I don't have to let the worry about others' reactions or possible judgment stop me. Everyone is entitled to their opinion and their feelings about a decision. Even if I choose something that upsets someone, it does not mean my decision was wrong.

I'm paying attention. I'm noticing. I'm doing something or making a choice and seeing what happens. I've made some simplistic and maybe even ridiculous baby steps, like cutting the watermelon differently just to see what would happen. Who would comment? Would somebody say something? Would anybody be upset? How would I feel about putting it out on the table? I over-explained too much. I still made sure that it was okay. And then, when no one got angry, I let the worry go. And you know what? It turned out fine. It turned out better than fine. People liked the shape of the watermelon.

I've made some really big decisions like choosing to go to Hawaii by myself, and although I spent a couple of weeks trying to decide to tell different people out of fear of how they were going to react, I still made a choice. And I'm excited! And I still have to tell myself I have the right to be excited. And I still have the right to have some worries.

Love,
Your True Self

**Armor**

If I wear the armor no one can see
The parts I hide
The anger
The hurt
The lack of confidence
The loneliness
The insecurity
The feeling of abandonment
The worry

But if I take it off they can see
The real me
My heart
My strength
My smile
My empathy
My desire to share
My worthiness
My kindness

**Who's On the Bus**

I'm driving a bus. I'm finally in the driver's seat
The little girl, who focused on abandonment, is now just along for the ride.
The teenager who didn't feel like she fit in is sitting near the back.
The young woman who didn't know if she was good enough is looking out the window.
The widow who was living in grief is now smiling as the view is passed by.
The college student who was figuring stuff out is curled up on the left.
The teacher who wondered if she was making a difference is checking on everyone.
I've stopped along the way to learn many lessons and meet new people.
I'm continuing on the path that's laid out, but now I'm choosing the map.

**You Get to Decide**

Decide when to go
Decide where to go
Decide where to stay
Decide what to do
Decide what to eat

Decide when to sleep
Decide who will go
Decide how long
Decide when to get up
Decide what to watch

It's all up to you
Your needs matter
Your wants matter
Your voice matters
Your opinion counts

---

What do your dreams want you to do or be?

Dear Little One,

I see how scared you are. I see how much you don't like being alone. I see how much confusion you have going on. I know you wonder why you're not at home. I know you're confused about where your dad has gone and who this new guy is. You are right to have all the feelings you have.

Someday, more of this will make sense to you. Someday you'll understand that you were always loved and that although you were sent to be at your grandparents' house, it wasn't because your mom didn't love you. She sent you there because she knew that was the safest place for you to be. She had to figure out who she was as a person first. She had to figure out how she could be a single mom. She had to figure out how to be in a relationship with a new person. And while all of that was going on with her you were a big part of her life. But it was exhausting. It was hard to be the only caretaker 24 hours a day 7 days a week, while trying to go to school and have a job. And with the knowledge she had, having you be with her parents was the best option for everyone. You formed such a relationship with them and have so many memories of being with them and at their house and at the camp. Your connection to your grandparents is phenomenal and such a blessing. Cherish that. Continue to soak up all of the love and the care and the lullabies and the comfort of the rocking chair every moment you can. And let your mom love you as she needs to in every way that's possible because she absolutely adores you. You are her greatest gift. She'll tell you later in life that you're a really good thing to come out of her first marriage.

Love,
Layla

## Escaping

I'm not escaping myself
I'm not abandoning myself
I'm not forgetting who I am
I'm also moving forward

I'm changing who's in the driver's seat
I'm learning the parts of me that have been hidden
I'm hiding other parts of me that no longer serve a purpose
I'm figuring out what makes me happy in this version of my soul
I'm experiencing new parts of my being to experience joy

I want to do more than survive
My past has made me who I am today
All of my ups and downs brought me to this place

I feel like I'm learning new pieces
To ask for help, to feel confident, to feel worthy
To not be put down by those that say I'm not smart enough
I do not listen when they say I'm too loud or I care too much

I'm learning my purpose and who I've always meant to be
Uncovering the layers and seeing all the parts
I need to love each component and shard of my soul

Thank you, Gramma and Grandpa,

Thank you for always being available to take care of me. To love me and be there for me when I needed it. I wish I had told you more when you were alive how much growing up with you meant to me. How many memories do I have of being at your house and at the camp? I always felt comfort, safety, and love when I was around both of you. The attention and care you gave me made me feel so special.

When I had children of my own, I wanted them to have the same feelings with their grandparents. I knew that connection was so important in making them into loving, compassionate people. Having my needs met and getting special treats was amazing.

I don't have a lot of memories of being little and being at home, and I don't know if it's because I spent more time at your house or because the times at your house were just more special. I think many of the things I do for self-care now, are things I had with you when I was little because my heart could still feel that calmness and peace and love. Having a special plate to have my French toast on in the morning, being by the water at the camp, making hot thimbleberry jam, singing lullabies and reading, taking a bath and putting on a cozy nightgown, frozen Milky Ways, and card games; all of these things bring me so much joy. All of these things connect with a memory of being with you.

I love you both so much. I am so grateful to Mom for living near you and having a relationship with you and allowing me to be taken care of and loved by you. I am blessed that you purchased the property by the lake, so that I have a place to go to feel connected to my soul and to God and to the memories of you. Thank you for building the camp so I can sit by the fire and spend the night. I know you have always watched over me and my boys.

Love,
Your Emy

**Safe and Secure**

Supported
Loved
Held
Safe
Secure
Taken care of

Baths given
Treats created
Songs sung
Stories read
Bedtime routine
Special blanket
Morning cuddles
Games played
Favorite meals

Taken Care of
Secure
Safe
Held
Loved
Supported

_____

*Who or what makes you feel safe and supported?*

Dear Emilie,

Forgiveness doesn't mean forgetting, and it doesn't mean that what somebody did was right. Forgiveness allows the person who was hurt to feel lighter and less pain. You can forgive someone when you know that they were doing the best they could with the knowledge they had in the experience they were having. Being able to go back and forgive people for saying things to you, treating you a certain way, or allowing you to feel something can be healing for both of you. Even if that person isn't here anymore, you can offer them forgiveness.

Maybe you also need to forgive yourself. Maybe a part of you also treated them poorly, or didn't let their voice be heard because of anger or confusion. Perhaps the stress they were under was so intense that it took over moments that should have been loving and turned them into chaos and confusion. Maybe the grief they felt from the losses they had already experienced was too intense for them to have joy and allow you to have a good time. Maybe they didn't even know what was affecting you because you got good at hiding your emotions. You never wanted anyone to be upset for fear that you would be abandoned, or left behind or not loved, and so you didn't tell anybody your fears and worries and anxiety.

Sheltering everybody from what you thought were negative emotions didn't allow people to connect with you fully and be able to help you through that, especially when you were little. You can't go back and change what happened, how people felt, or what emotions you experienced, but you can feel some understanding of what others were going through at the same time. You can have empathy for grief and loss and anger because you've felt it, too. You can still love all of these people from your past even if they also hurt you or made you feel unworthy of love. You can be upset and mad because of experiences you had or didn't get to have because of what someone else was going through.

Maybe nobody realized that you felt unworthy, unconfident, and doubtful of your dreams, hopes, and wishes. Maybe the fact that you wrote lots of things in your journals instead of having conversations with people made it hard for them to love you in the way you needed because they just didn't know. Maybe you weren't meant to take on any of their pain. Maybe you weren't meant to feel hurt and unsafe. Maybe you weren't supposed to question your value. Maybe you were just supposed to be you. Maybe you were supposed to just have fun and see the joy. Maybe you took on problems that weren't yours to solve.

But you are forgiven for that. You did the best you could with the knowledge you had. You did the best you could with the people around you who are also going through difficult things. You have always been the best version of yourself. You have always been loved. Even if people are angry, upset, annoyed with you or something you've done, it doesn't mean that you're not loved. Even if somebody leaves your life and is no longer connected with you, it doesn't mean that you're not worthy. Even if you offer things that cost people money, it doesn't mean that you're selfish.

Love,
Forgiveness

**Forgiving**

Does it mean it's right?
No.
Does it mean you forget?
No.
Does it mean it won't happen again?
No.
Does it have to come from them?
No.

Will it make you feel better?
Yes.
Does it help with healing?
Yes.
Can you keep it to yourself?
Yes.
Does it mean you can let go?
Yes.
Is it really for you, not them?
Yes.

---

What do you need to be forgiven for?
What do you need to forgive of others?

Dear Emy,

I want you to see that I allowed you to be safe and loved at home by being absent. You did not need the version of me that I sometimes lived. You deserved a loving, sober, and happy dad. I could not always be that. My love for you didn't ever change. I was always ready to protect and fight for you. I also knew you were loved and taken care of even when I wasn't there. I'm sorry you thought you were the reason that I stayed away.

Love,
B

**Little Me**

I wish I'd known about the depression.
I needed the shift in my perspective.
That it was never me.
I wasn't the one to blame.
It wasn't my fault.
I was just a little girl caught up in the chaos.
I was the product of love that didn't work out.
I was protected by not being seen.
I couldn't be me out of fear of hurting someone.
I wanted to choose, but I worried about my mom, too.
I was too little to have to be everything for everyone.

Emilie,

Marking your subtraction problems wrong was discouraging and hurtful, and I can see that it has damaged your self-confidence, belief in your worth, and faith in your abilities in school. I'm sorry for how that has affected you all these years. I wish I could go back and have a one-on-one conversation with you in the hallway, and tell you how smart you were and that the answers you put on that paper were correct. You are brilliant, intelligent, worthy, and loved. I see the joy in your eyes when we do school work, and you help others. I love watching you run to the library to be able to check out books. Having something that comes easy to you doesn't always apply to the rest of your life and it can make other things seem super hard.

I want you to know that you probably have something like dyslexia, where spelling is really challenging for you. Perhaps it's because you have a hard time visualizing things and so you can't see the words and maybe you don't hear the sounds the same as other people, and so spelling might be something that's always difficult for you. Don't give up on it, continue to write, continue to learn, and believe in yourself—because you've got this.

Chemistry is tough for a lot of people. There are formulas and concentration while figuring things out, problem-solving, and new vocabulary. It is like learning a foreign language. But I see your willingness to learn. I see your ability to help other people. I know how much you care for other students in this school. I know you want to do well in this class. I am so happy that you asked for more explanation and more information about things so that you can try to find a way to fit it into your brain.

I appreciate your work and the time you take to learn a subject that I'm passionate about but that you probably don't need and won't need in your life. I am proud of you for taking a challenging class, helping other students study, and giving them study tips. I love that you bring community into each classroom you walk into, and I love witnessing you outside of school on the swim team.

Your grade in this class does not define your worth, value, or intelligence. Not everyone's brain learns the same material in the same way at the same rate. Your brain is no different. Your connections to others in this class are more important than knowing the chemical equations for certain things like ammonia. Your teamwork for your lab projects with your partner and the skills and friendship you're developing will be so much more valuable than measuring liquids into a beaker. Your ability to make others smile and feel good is immensely valuable. Don't let anybody shut down your light because of a test score or the grade on your final exam.

I need you to see how smart and talented you are and how much you are loved by your peer group and accepted in the school. However, you don't demonstrate how good you are at math and don't always complete your homework; you're asking for help from your friends and trying to learn the material. I can see that, and I should never have told you that you were not a good math student.

I know that everybody can be a good math student, and I see the skills that you have and that you are a problem solver. Someday, I hope you realize that the comments we make as teachers don't always reflect what you are as a person. Telling you that day in the hallway when your mom asked about you taking physics, that "you weren't a good math student" was me protecting myself. I believed that if you took physics, you weren't going to do well, and that would reflect poorly on me as a teacher. If I have students who don't do well, it means I'm not teaching well, and that's not the case. I am teaching the material and you're not in the right headspace or soul space to be receiving what I'm teaching.

You need to trust and believe in yourself, and continue asking for help.

From,
Your Teachers

**Seasonal Emotions**

Recharge in the winter
Renew the spring
Rejuvenate in the summer
Rest in the fall

Feel the joy and happiness
Feel the sadness and anger
Feel your emotions
Feel the full expression

Dear True You,

I think grief and the loss of a partner is a mixed blessing. There's no way to know if I would have become this version of me if Steve were still alive, but I don't think so. I think being married for twenty years, co-parenting, and working full-time keeps you in a certain version. Because of Steve's death, I became a widow and a single parent and was able to retire. Becoming this version of me has been a long road and I know the love and support that he gave me for all of those years we were together is important to shaping who I am today.

I'm able to move forward and find new love because of the love he gave me. I'm able to heal and not be stuck grieving because of the love he gave me and the importance of our relationship. I'm able to be a parent to the kids because of the skills we learned together as parents. I'm able to learn what I want and what I need and make decisions because of all of the decisions we had to make together and that we got to make together. There's such a blessing in the life we had, the life we shared, and the grief that I went through after his death. The moments of grief that I will continue to go through are so important in discovering who I am and who I want to be.

Love,
Grief and Loss

**Both**

I'm in love with you
I'm in love with him
I'll always love both

My heart has space for you
My heart has space for him
My heart will keep you both

I can love the you you are
I can love him as he was
I can love you both differently

I won't let you go
I can't let him go
I will always keep both of you

God gave me you
God gave me him
God knew I needed you both

Dear Emilie,

You may need to trust that more than one thing can be true at one time.

Parents can be doing the absolute best they can, and you can still get hurt. Just because everyone is going through something doesn't mean they are processing the events or emotions the same way. You can have a great life and feel that you were abandoned.

You can know what you want but struggle to make decisions. You certainly have hopes, dreams, and things that you want to have, but you are also worried about what others will think or how your choices will affect others.

You can be together with somebody and yet feel alone. Maybe you're physically in the same space, but emotionally, you're worrying, having fears, or doubts even though you're safe and loved.

You can have faith that everything is going to work out and be fine, but you can still be anxious, worried, and fearful about the situation.

You know that you can have grief about the loss of somebody and still feel absolute joy. You know that sometimes a song will make you cry, and other times you'll just smile. You can be angry at people that are no longer here. You can be so sad and upset that people have died and yet focus on the memories and the good times with those people.

You can enjoy something that is difficult. You can not want something because it's too easy. Is it there to teach you a lesson and to show you something new? Wanting to take a leap and do something different than you've done before doesn't mean that you have to be 100% confident. You can be nervous that it's not going to work out. You can be scared. But you can also have faith and trust. You can make a decision that you believe with your heart and know to be true and then, in a few days, decide that it's no longer right and change your mind.

Let all of the feelings be felt. Let all experiences reveal more than one way of seeing what happened. Learn different methods to do something. One of your most significant skills as a teacher was understanding that everybody thinks differently, and that what works for one kid might not work for another. You believed that asking for help was a strength. You felt everyone could learn if given the right tools in the right situation and time. You now need to know those things for yourself. You can ask for help, and it doesn't diminish your independence. You can use a different tool or timeline than someone else and succeed. You can choose to love the way it works for you.

Love,
Dichotomy

## Dichotomy

Grief and joy
Love and loneliness
Anxiousness and excitement
Good and bad
Tired and enthusiastic
Random and real
Confusion and understanding
Fear and anticipation
Single and together
Rest and productivity
Hunger and fulfillment
Dreams and successes
Hopes and trust
Belief and curiosity
Nervousness and trust
Light and dark
Scary and fun
Safe and playful

Dear Emilie,

Be you always. You don't need to put up a shield that blocks the real you and only allows others to see the shadows and forms of who you really are. Come out and see what you desire. Let the trust flow that you'll set boundaries. You have permission to seek joy, be happy, and feel love and self-love. I want you to feel your breath, laughter, and smiles and remember the love and the hugs. Love all parts of you. Your layers will always be a part of you, but they don't have to be the focus. Spend time being all of you, not a role, not a teacher, not because of who you're with, just you. Lay down and feel connected with the layers of your soul. Be curious about all the parts of who you've been, are now, and will become. All parts are sacred and flow together. Be you always. Speak your truth because you have the right to be happy, seen, and heard. Your desires matter. See who you have always been and who you do not need to try to be. You can just be you. You are loved. You are valuable. You are wanted.

Love,
You Now

## Be My Own Mom

Hug me every day
Love me unconditionally
Feed me my favorite foods
Have expectations
Provide emotional support
Be reliable and present
Honor my needs
See how I'm unique
Tell me I'm special and worthy
Pray for me
Give me alone time
Buy me presents
Honor me with celebrations
Tuck me in and sing a lullaby
Say I love you often

---

What did you need to hear from your parents?
What would you offer yourself as your own loving parent?

**Boat**

There's a boat that goes to my dreams.
Am I worthy to get on it?
Who says I deserve a ticket?
What if it crashes and sinks?
Can I ask for help?
What if I do get on?

I am worthy of my dreams.
I do have experience and skills.
I will never be alone on the boat.
My friends will always be there.
It's okay to wear a life jacket.
It's okay to ask for support.

Everyone is on a boat to their dreams, too.
Everyone makes a choice.
Others ask for help,
Others wear life jackets.
Others have different experiences.

---

*What does confidence need you to know?*

Dear Emilie,

I'm so glad you're choosing to go to Hawaii. This is something you've dreamed about for almost your entire lifetime. You've made a big decision. You're going to travel by yourself to a place you've wanted to go since you were a little girl. A place you thought you'd go with your family. A place you thought you'd go to celebrate your 25th wedding anniversary. A place you thought you'd go when you hit a weight loss goal. And now you're going to go by yourself as a celebration of becoming a version of yourself who does scary things because you want to. Because you can. Because your wants and desires matter. Because you matter. Because you're worthy. Because you deserve to have fun and pleasure. Even though your life path changed, you still get to do fun things.

Choosing to go alone and not bring your kids is a huge decision. You always want to support them, be there for them, and give them the best experiences. But this is your dream, not theirs. Spending a significant amount of money on yourself is going to be very different, but it shows what's possible. At this point in your life, with all you've done financially, you deserve to spend some of it on yourself on something that might be frivolous in some people's eyes.

You know, for you, this dream being brought to fruition allows other dreams to also come to fruition. This allows your dreams of sharing your experiences with other widows, creating books and materials that help others heal, and speaking on stages about your journey to healing and becoming this version of you to all come true. You don't need to know how. You don't need to know the logistics. You don't have to have all of the fears and worries. You can do something because you want to. Plain and simple. You don't need any other reasons.

You don't need permission from anyone. You don't need to think about who this will hurt or how others will feel. You don't need to worry about the financial part. You can keep yourself safe. You can come back if that's necessary. You can use this time to focus on your mind, body, and spirit. This can be your retreat. This can be time for your body to heal. This can be a time for reflection and meditation. This can be a time to work through all kinds of emotions like grief, joy, and anger.

It will be good for everyone to see a newer version of you—maybe a version that they have never seen because you've been hiding it. This will allow others to see that you do have wants and that you can fulfill those wants on your own. You can feel the support of others. You are experiencing the joy of allowing your dreams to be reality. This is good. This shows your children that, as a mom, you can do things on your own. This shows your parents that you are a grown up and can do things on your own. This shows your partner that you are independent and can do things on your own. This shows your business that you can earn money and pay for things on your own. This shows the little girl in you that dreams come true. This honors the life you and Steve had together. This honors the highest version of yourself.

This might be scary. You might have fears about this. You might cry. You might feel sad. You might get lonely. You will miss having others with you. You will grieve. But you know love and grief coexist. Joy and happiness coexist. Fun and anxiety coexist. Memories and the present coexist.

Others might judge you. Others might think you're being selfish. Others might think it's a waste of money. Others might think it's unfair. Your kids might feel left behind. Your family might feel forgotten. Your partner might feel lonely.

The excitement and nervousness you're feeling are things you can experience often. It doesn't have to be as extravagant as a week-long vacation to a tropical island. It can be choosing what you want to have for dinner or what you think would make a perfect afternoon, choosing a movie to go to, or what book you want to read. It can allow others to help you and support you. It can be setting boundaries and saying no without guilt. It can be using your voice and being heard without feeling you're too loud. You can live with your whole heart and allow it to be a strength.

Go and have fun. Be there! See who you are when you are by yourself. Do things you want to do when you want to do them. Pick things that make you light up. Choose foods that sound good. Sleep when you want to sleep. Sit on the beach and read a book. Get up and watch the sunrise. Stay up and watch the sunset. Lay in the water in your bikini. Eat pineapple and fresh fish. Write in your journal and process the emotions that you're feeling. Lay in your bed and watch a movie with sand on your feet from the ocean.

Do you. Be you. Feel you. Love you.

Love,
Your Dreams

**Hawaii**

A place I've wanted to go
A place of my dreams
A place of peace and tranquility
A place to be immersed in water
A place to heal and grieve
A place of self-acceptance
A place to be unapologetically me
A place to travel alone
A place showing dreams come true
A place proving I am worthy
A place to make choices
A place I didn't get to go
A place I'm now choosing for me

Dear Emilie,

When you go back and think about all of the things you felt for the past 49 years, you assume that you were the only one feeling those things... but you're wrong. Many people have felt unworthy, and others have felt unloved or abandoned. Everyone experiences confusion and the unknown. All children are trying to make sense of the world. You have chosen not to share your experiences and your journey because you're worried about what others are going to think or feel about your words.

These are your words. This is your experience. This is how you journeyed through the world and the relationships you've been part of. Everyone in your life was working through something. Nothing anyone felt or believed, other than love, was because of you. Everyone was doing the best they could with the knowledge they had. You have done the best you could with the knowledge you had.

Love,
Knowledge

**Cloves of Garlic**

I am a head of garlic
many cloves are part of my soul
each one part of the whole
separate multiple cloves
peeled simultaneously
all remain a part of who I am
regardless of the version I show
I live with joy
everything fits together

## Choices

I can choose now.
I can decide now.
I can focus on my wants.
I can have my dreams.
I can have my desires.
I can choose me.

My choices don't hurt others.
My love is felt even if I'm gone.
My loved ones don't feel abandoned.
My love is strong and unconditional.

They love me when I make choices.
They want me to decide sometimes.
They want me to feel love too.
They help me live my dreams.

---

*What does your intuition tell you to choose?*

**Who are we?**

Who is she?
She sees a lot of clients.
She stopped teaching.
She does more than one service.
She got out of debt.
She offers one-on-one and group work.
She charges for her services.
She offers both free and not free items.
She is capable and valuable.
She promotes herself.
She is happy and filled with joy.
She takes risks.
She makes changes.
She is also a mom and wife.

Who am I?
I see lots of clients.
I stopped teaching.
I do more than one service.
I am out of debt.
I offer both one-on-one and group services.
I charge for my services.
I offer both free and fee items.
I am capable and valuable.
I promote myself.
I am happy and filled with joy.
I take risks.
I adjust and make changes
I am also a mom and partner.
I am her.

Repressed anger,

I know you're there. What power do you hold? What will happen if I let you out? Will you explode? How long will you last? Will you be in all areas of my life? Will it be rage, sadness, tears, throwing stuff, or screaming? Do I need to do this release alone? In therapy? With a group of friends holding baseball bats around a fire playing loud music?

Is it about grief and the unfairness of Tacy's death way too young, or Steve's death too young, and leaving me a widow and single parent? Bruce's death without enough answers? Is it about feeling abandoned and never wanting to pass that on to the boys? Is it about not ever letting you show up for all these years, stuffing you inside whenever you rose up and tried to get out - afraid that if I showed you, people would get upset and leave?

Why are you coming out now? Why do you need to be seen in here? Why can't you stay hidden behind some other pieces like sadness, grief, people-pleasing, and anxiety? Why do you want a more significant piece of my life right now? Why do you feel now is your time to finally be an emotion I accept and work with?

I don't feel like I know you. I don't know what to do with you. I only know how to yell and walk away, maybe slam a door. I know to put on music to keep you quiet. The music blocks you out, and then you'll go away. I know that if I choose to leave and walk away, no one will follow - no one will come after me, and that's scary.

So what do I do? Do I let you out? Do I feel all of you? Do I allow myself to feel the pressure in my chest, the racing heartbeat, my hands in fists, the jumpy feeling in my legs, the urge to yell, swear, and scream, and the desire to swing an axe and cut down a tree? Do I yell the words I want, the words I want to hear?

I'm here.
I'm heard.
I'm seen.
I'm worthy.
I'm loved.
I matter.

Do I scream things for the baby who listens to the fights? For the 4-year-old left on the steps feeling it was her fault that he didn't pick her up again? For the child who was taken care of by her grandparents so often? For the sister who struggled with mental health?

For the parent who abused the friend in high school? For the student teacher supervisor who showed me how not to teach? For the reasons I had to call CPS so many times? For the unfairness of miscarriage? For misunderstanding and not getting forgiveness? For untimely deaths? For not talking about money concerns? For being a single-parent widow? For cancer, brain tumors, and unexplained deaths? For condescending comments about me? For not becoming and believing in myself?

And who do I get to be angry with? My mom, Bruce, my dad, my sisters, Steve, my kids, Chris, God, the government, kids I taught, their parents, money, my body, world issues, prejudices, deaths, clutter, self-doubt, the weather, illnesses?

What if you're too much? What if you're too overwhelming? What if I can't function in other areas because I'm too focused on you and your feelings? Do I go away to process you? Do I tell people you're going to be my focus? Do I pick a time so you don't come out at the wrong or inconvenient time?

How do I accept you and allow you to be here?

From,
Confused Me

**Unsure and Confused**

It's a new feeling
It's unknown
It feels weird
It feels difficult
It's scary
It's been hidden
It's confusing

It's shaking inside
It's pressure building
It's hot
It's a violet color
It's a racing heart
It's tight fists
It's closed eyes
It's a heavy feeling

Dear Emilie,

Honor the gift of self-discovery and learning to see inwardly, be focused on how decisions feel in your body and soul, and go within to see the possibilities without fear or judgment. Go for it. Live big. Climb across the bridges. Go where you haven't been before.

Be you! The real authentic you. Do not fear the unknown or the success. It's okay to want to be successful. It's okay to be known. It's okay to be loud and fun. It's okay to want to help everyone. It's okay to be you.

Look into the future without worry, fear, or anxiety. Look into the future with anticipation, joy, excitement, and hope. See the good that will come. Focus on that good. See the beauty in being a leader, an entrepreneur, a speaker, a SoulCollage® facilitator, a partner, a mom, a grandma, a grief coach, an author, a podcaster, a beachgoer, a writer, a yogi, a reader, a traveler, and a walker.

Believe that you have the freedom to do and say what your heart wants. Leave the fears and worries behind. Focus on the present moment. Trust yourself. Trust that you are loved unconditionally. Focus on what has worked in the past, the easy yes, and the times you trusted your voice. Speak your truth. Follow your intuition. Trust your instincts to do what makes you feel good, even if it's something similar to your past or seems scary. Put yourself first without worries about others' thoughts or possible judgment. You are loved. Others also have the right to say yes or no.

Express your anger, rage, hurt, and feelings of unworthiness or abandonment. Throw stuff, stomp, and scream. Release it all from your body because it can be healing and reforming. You can't heal what you won't accept, and it also won't let go. Release the fear of judgment. No one has the right to make you do something you don't want to do and that you don't feel in your heart. Your ideas, hopes, and dreams are valid.

Stop putting up walls and society rules around your freedom to be you. Come out of your shell. Stop hiding behind the past and worrying about the future. See your ideas, dreams, and creativity as help for somebody.

You don't help or teach anyone if you don't put anything out into the world. No one can see inside your head or your journals. No one can support you or help you if you don't let them try. No one's judgment of you changes who you are or your worth. You are always valuable to the world because God made you.

Take the leap. Take the risk you fear. See what happens. You might find it's fun. You might be successful. You might love what you're doing. You might help someone else smile, feel joy, love, or empathy because you let go of the fear and share yourself with the world.

You are a teacher, a healer, and a guide for others. Your story is a survival guide for someone else. Your ability to create, write, and share is unique. Never let self-doubt get in the way of being who you were put here to be. Always allow your purpose to come through. Your love is your light. Your love is your passion. Your love is your purpose. Love with your mind, body, and spirit always.

Be the you you were meant to be.

Love,
Confidence

**Rock Climber**

Look at her way up there!
How did she get there?
Did she have support?
Did someone help her?
Was she offered a rope?
Who put the carabiners in the wall?
How many handholds did she use?
Did she learn to come back down?
Does she know how to repel?
How are her knot-tying skills?

She climbed.
She worked hard.
She trusted the adults in her life.
She believed in her self-worth.
She knew she could do hard things.
She remembered times she had been successful.
She asked for and accepted help.
She learned skills that will help her in the future.
She knew she could try again or start over.
She trusted the ropes that were given to her.

Dear Emilie,

I am always here for you. I have always been here. I will always be here. Trust in the journey. Believe in my plan. Know you are worthy, loved, and wanted. Reflect and see the times when you were your authentic self, and you put yourself into the world how loved you were. Remember all of the people that have chosen to love you over your lifetime. Be prepared that as you choose, people may fall away, but other people may come into your life.

This is who we were meant to be. This is who you will always be. This part of your soul has been waiting for you to accept, trust, and know that now is the time. Make the decision. Figure out your wants. Share your passion with the world. No one else's opinion, judgment, or experience can change what deeply motivates you and makes you feel like the absolute best version of yourself.

You deserve to be happy. You deserve to experience love. You deserve to feel your innate, unchangeable worth. You were made to be a teacher and share your knowledge and experience with the world. You were made to connect with others, but not sacrifice your connection with yourself. Be you. Be you unapologetically. Be love. Be hope. Be the you you want your children to see.

You are worthy. You were created worthy. Nothing you can do will change your worthiness because it came from me. It doesn't matter what kind of daughter, sister, friend, partner, wife, mom, or employee you are. It doesn't matter how much you help others; spend time alone, clean your house, gather with others, choose activities, pray to, and honor your mind, body, and spirit. It doesn't matter if you have self-doubt, feel fat, believe you're not confident, experience confusion, wonder about other people, or try to please people.

Nothing you can say, believe, or think, will change your worthiness. I chose to create you and put you here now for a purpose. You don't need to know why. You don't need to know how long you'll be here. You don't need to see how you've changed other people. You don't need to be afraid of what others will think.

Everything is already perfect and the way it's meant to be. Be still and know that I am God.

Love,
God

**Dear me,**

I see your struggles.
I see your grief.
I see your self-doubt.
I see your health worries.

Give it all to God.
Stop the worry or fear.
Pray.
Know.
Believe.
Trust.

You are perfect.
You are worthy.
You are loved.

Focus on now.
Focus on gratitude.
Focus on hope.

You're ready for the journey.
You're worthy of this life.
You're given all you need.
You've been chosen.

**My Obituary**

Born to two parents, adopted by a third
Sister to two girls; parent to three boys
Wife to one man; partner to another, love
A high school graduate, college and masters
A teacher, then author and entrepreneur
A woman mixed with grief and joy
A lover of water, agates, books, and journals
A healer, mentor, and guide

---

*What do you want to be written in your obituary?*
*How do you want to be remembered?*

## Acknowledgments

Thank you to all those who have unconditionally loved me along the way, especially my mom, dad, Bruce, gramma, grandpa, Steve, Michael, Brian, Matthew, Skylar, and Chris. (I'm afraid to start listing people in case I forget anyone.) I am so blessed to have many families, including the Hawkins, the Langes, the Andersons, the Lancours (importantly Doug, Julie, and Stacy), and now the Toutants, to accept and love me. I have always felt like a part of your family and never like a traditional 'step' or 'in-law'!

Thank you to all my amazing friends who will listen without judgment and offer a hug and understanding—the friends from elementary school, middle and high school, college, Calumet Public Schools, Hancock Public Schools, the CCISD, church, and because of Calm Water Writing. Especially to Stacy, Leslie, and Doug for always being there no matter what time of day or the circumstances.

Thank you to the healers I've experienced who have provided healing sessions, sound healing and biofield tuning, myofascial release, Chakradance, massages, coaching, healing touch, therapy, and meditation. Thank you Emily, Lisa, Nikki, Zoe, Jenny, Clare, Lisa, Kaela, and the Soulful Women.

Thank you to all the others who are grieving and sharing their grief journeys with me. I believe that grief and joy coexist.

Thank you to the medical professionals I have worked with for counseling, chiropractic care, depression, anxiety, ADHD, and my physical health.

Thank you to God and my faith. I trust in Your plan.

## About the Author

Emilie is a mom, retired educator, and reader. Professionally, she is a journaling mentor, grief guide, and author. Family, friends, and faith are most important to her. She is outgoing but loves quiet time on the beach with God, her camera, and a journal.

After her husband passed away in 2017, she started a blog, grieffaithandfinances.com, and a podcast, 'Grief is Random and Real.' As an author, she has published four books. Two are about her journey through grief, healing and learning to love again. Another is about the miracles she's experienced. In 2023, she released New Growth Poetry. Emilie has also created multiple courses, workbooks, and journals.

After retiring from a career in special education, Emilie started "Calm Water Writing," a company that offers healing and soul connection through journaling. Her primary work is with other widows to allow the discovery that grief and joy coexist. Emilie trusts that journaling connects with parts of our souls and deepens the journey we are all on. She offers long-form journaling, grief healing, bullet journaling, and SoulCollage® in one-on-one sessions, classes, and courses.

Emilie also spends her free time with her partner, picking agates and photographing nature, mainly in the beautiful Upper Peninsula of Michigan and Lake Superior.

*Also by Emilie Lancour*

"It's Okay to be Okay;
Finding Joy through Grief" (2020)

"A Cup of Miracles" (2022)

"It's Okay to Love Again" (2023)

"New Growth Poetry" (2023)

"My Spouse Died, Now What?" (2023)

"Healing through Holiday Grief" (2023)

"Grief and Joy Coexist Journal" (2024)

"A Year of Journaling with One Sentence" (2024)

"G is for Grief, A Coloring Book and Journal" (2025)

www.ingramcontent.com/pod-product-compliance
Lightning Source LLC
Chambersburg PA
CBHW020541030426
42337CB00013B/929